slow cooking
just for yourself

slow cooking
just for yourself

catherine atkinson

foulsham
LONDON • NEW YORK • TORONTO • SYDNEY

foulsham

Capital Point, 33 Bath Road, Slough, Berkshire, SL1 3UF,
England

Foulsham books can be found in all good bookshops
and direct from www.foulsham.com

ISBN 978-0-572-03150-3

Last reprinted 2012

Cover photograph by Fresh Food Images

A CIP record for this book is available from the British Library

Printed in Great Britain by CPI Group (UK) Ltd, Croydon CR0 4YY

Contents

Introduction

Whether you live alone or are simply having a solitary night in, cooking can be a chore and it may be the last thing you feel like at the end of the day. It's all too easy to dash out for a takeaway or settle for a chilled ready-made meal from a packet. Slow cooking is the perfect way to create flavour-packed meals with the minimum effort and fuss. Ideal for soups, casseroles, vegetables and desserts, this method of cooking means that you can prepare meals in advance and simply leave them unattended to cook for as many hours as they need.

The basic principle behind the slow cooker is that it cooks food slowly at a low constant temperature. This has many advantages. One of the greatest is that it develops and enhances the flavour of food, while retaining its texture. It brings out the sweetness in fruit and vegetables and makes even the toughest meat meltingly tender – in fact, the less expensive cuts are better suited to slow cooking. Slow cookers are also environmentally friendly; their low wattage consumes about the same amount of electricity as a light bulb. A bonus is that food is unlikely to burn or over-dry; if you're out for the day, an extra hour of cooking won't ruin your recipe, so there's no need to worry if you get home a little later than planned. The principles of slow cooking are incredibly simple, but do have a look at the following few pages before you begin.

All the recipes in this book have been created to use a range of ingredients that are easy to buy on a small scale. They are designed for one, but many make two servings – one to serve straight away and one that can be jazzed up the following day (you'll find plenty of suggestions for this), or frozen for a later date. There are mouthwatering meals to suit every occasion from light lunches and midweek meals to delectable desserts. Solo eating will never be the same again!

Choosing a slow cooker

*S*low cookers now come in a huge range of colours, shapes, sizes and prices and these factors need to be considered before you make your choice.

Appearance is the first thing you'll notice; you'll find contemporary stainless steel, vibrant coloured and pristine-looking white models as well as the rustic-looking cream versions. Originally only round slow cookers were available; these are excellent for soup and casserole making and for cooking puddings in basins and cakes in round tins. The more modern oval version is a better buy if you entertain often as it's perfect for pot-roasting larger joints of meat and is also good for cooking loaf-shaped cakes and pâtés. The heat-resistant lid may be ceramic or toughened glass. The advantage of the latter is that you can monitor the food's progress without having to lift the lid and lose precious heat.

The size of slow cookers ranges from a tiny 600 ml/1 pt/2½ cup cooking pot to a massive 6.5 litre/11¼ pt/27¾ cup one. I have found the ideal size to be 1.5 litres/2½ pt/6 cups; a large enough capacity for two portions, but small enough to ensure that food such as portions of fish or meat will fit snugly inside and be covered by the cooking liquid.

Using and caring for your slow cooker

Because slow cooker models vary, make sure you read the manufacturer's guide book before using yours for the first time. Some slow cookers need to be preheated before you start cooking; others advise against heating the slow cooker when empty. You should also check to see whether yours is dishwasher proof and whether it can be used under the grill (broiler) and in the oven, in the microwave or the freezer.

Before use, wash the ceramic cooking pot in hot soapy water, rinse well and dry. You may notice a slight odour as the slow cooker heats up; this is caused by the burning off of manufacturing residues and should disappear after the first few uses. Don't worry if the glaze on the ceramic becomes slightly crazed; this is perfectly normal.

You'll notice that the recipes here advise using hot (not boiling) water and stock when adding it straight to the cooking pot; never pour boiling liquid into the cold cooking pot (you can do so when it is already warm or hot) or plunge it into cold water immediately after use as this could crack it. Remember that it is an electrical appliance, so the outer casing should only be wiped clean and never immersed in or filled with water.

When following a recipe, bear in mind that every model is slightly different and, even when using the same settings, some will cook faster than others. For this reason a range of cooking times is given; you may need to use the shorter or the longer time, or somewhere between the two. Remember, also, that if you use a larger slow cooker than the 1.5 litre/2½ pt/6 cup model I used for testing, there may be more evaporation of liquid. After trying a few recipes, you will know whether your slow cooker is faster or slower and you will be able to adjust the recipe cooking times accordingly.

During cooking, steam condenses on the lid of the slow cooker, then trickles back into the pot, helping to retain heat and reduce strong cooking smells. Unless a recipe tells you to stir a dish part-way through cooking, it should be left undisturbed and you should avoid lifting the lid.

Cooking times

*T*he cooking temperatures and settings vary on different models, but most have four settings: Off, Low, High and Auto. Some models have an additional Medium setting. At the lowest temperature the food will barely simmer, at the highest it will cook at just below boiling point or boil very gently.When set to Auto, the cooking temperature will build up to High, then remain at this temperature for an hour or so before automatically switching to Low. Some flexibility can be introduced to the total cooking time by adjusting the temperature setting. Some foods however, such as poultry and cakes, should always be cooked on High or Auto for at least the first hour of cooking. For dishes such as soups, braises and casseroles, the cooking can be shortened or extended to suit your needs by changing the temperature setting. As a rough guide, the cooking time on Low is about double that of High.

Low	*Auto or Medium*	*High*
6–8 hours	4–6 hours	3–4 hours
8–10	6–8 hours	5–6 hours

Slow cooker safety

*T*he slow cooker is an extremely safe appliance, but common-sense precautions should be followed. Although it cooks at a low temperature, the outer casing, lid and the food inside the slow cooker may get extremely hot, so you should always use oven gloves when removing the ceramic cooking pot. Stand the slow cooker on a heat-resistant surface when in use, not near the edge where it might accidentally get knocked off, and make sure that the mains lead is tucked safely behind it. Take extra care that it's out of reach if you have young children or inquisitive pets living or staying with you.

Slow cookers cook food at a relatively low heat – around 90°C/195°F on the Low setting to about 150°C/300°F on the High setting. Bacteria in food is destroyed at 74°C/165°F, so as long as it's cooked for the correct time, the temperature of the slow cooker will ensure that the food is safe to eat. You should take care, however, not to reduce the cooking temperature:

- Do not lift the lid during the cooking time unless the recipe specifies this.

- Make sure that ingredients are at room temperature when you start and never add frozen or part-frozen foods.

- Increase the cooking time slightly when the kitchen temperature is extremely cold, for example if you are cooking overnight.

- Avoid placing the slow cooker in a draughty place or near an open window.

Always check that meat is thoroughly cooked, particularly poultry and pork. A meat thermometer is a good investment if you cook portions or joints of meat as it will ensure they are sufficiently cooked without drying out and loosing moistness.

Slow cooking hints and tips

- If you need to lift the lid during cooking other than when I have specified in a recipe (to add a forgotten ingredient, for example), add an extra 15 minutes' cooking time to make up for the heat loss.

- Remember that there is less evaporation in the slow cooker than in conventional cooking so, when adapting your own recipes, reduce the liquid content by about a third.

- Alcohol evaporates more slowly in the slow cooker, so use only a small amount or the flavour may be overpowering.

- Root vegetables such as carrots, swede (rutabaga) and turnips take longer to cook than meat as the liquid simmers rather than boils. These should be cut into smallish even-sized chunks before adding to the cooking pot. If possible, place them at the bottom of the cooking pot, which is the hottest part, and make sure that they are completely immersed in liquid.

- Vegetables with a high water content such as pumpkins, squashes and courgettes (zucchini) will cook quickly, so add them towards the end of the cooking time.

- Frozen vegetables such as peas and sweetcorn should be thawed before adding (for speed, put them in a colander under cool running water). Once added, they'll take about 15 minutes to cook.

- Ordinary long-grain rice doesn't cook well in the slow cooker, but easy-cook (converted) rice, also known as 'parboiled', will cook to perfection. It has been steamed under pressure, ensuring the grains remain separate and making it difficult to overcook. Easy-cook brown, easy-cook basmati and easy-cook Italian (risotto) rices are also available.

- Both ordinary and easy-cook pastas can be used in the slow cooker, but the latter gives better results. Pasta made from 100% durum wheat will retain its shape and texture better than egg pasta.

- When cooking pâtés, cakes or desserts in tins or dishes in the slow cooker, always make sure that they will fit first as most cooking pots taper slightly towards the base. Place the tin or dish on an upturned saucer or a metal pastry (paste) cutter, so that the simmering water can circulate underneath and all around.

- Fresh herbs added at the beginning of long cooking will loose their colour and pungency. Use dried herbs at the start of cooking and add fresh ones towards the end.

Notes on the recipes

- Do not mix metric, imperial and American measures. Follow one set only.

- American terms are given in brackets.

- The ingredients are listed in the order in which they are used in the recipe.

- All spoon measurements are level: 1 tsp = 5 ml; 1 tbsp = 15 ml.

- Eggs are medium unless otherwise stated. If you use a different size, adjust the amount of liquid added to obtain the right consistency.

- Always wash, peel, core and seed, if necessary, fresh foods before use. Ensure that all produce is as fresh as possible and in good condition.

- The use of strongly flavoured ingredients such as garlic, chilli and ginger depends on personal taste and quantities can be adjusted accordingly.

- All cooking times are approximate and are intended as a guide only. Get to know your slow cooker; you will soon know if it cooks a little faster or slower than the times given here.

- Can and packet sizes are approximate and will depend on the particular brand.

- Vegetarian recipes are marked with a $\curlyvee$ symbol. Those who eat fish but not meat will find plenty of additional recipes containing seafood to enjoy. Some vegetarian recipes contain dairy products; omit them or substitute with a vegetarian alternative if you prefer. Recipes may also use processed foods, and vegetarians should check the specific product labels to be certain of their suitability, especially items such as pastry (paste), breads, biscuits (cookies) and cakes, stock, stock cubes, soups and sauces, jellies (jello) or set desserts, ice cream and chocolate products. Some alcoholic drinks also use animal-derived products in their production.

Soups and pâtés

No canned, packet or carton variety can rival a bowl of delicious home-made soup made with fresh ingredients and usually at a fraction of the price. In this chapter, you'll find classic soups from all round the world, including French Onion, Spanish Chorizo and Goulash Soup with Dumplings. Many are suitable for vegetarians and recipes such as Winter Lentil Soup and Mexican Bean Chowder contain pulses, which are both filling and a great source of protein. All can be served as light lunch or supper dishes, or complemented with bread to make a substantial main course.

The secret of a successful soup often lies in a well-flavoured stock, so if you haven't the time or inclination to make your own, choose a good-quality commercial variety and take care not to over-season as some already have a high salt content.

There are many easy ways to make a soup look extra special: a swirl of cream, crème fraîche or yoghurt, some grated Cheddar or Gruyère cheese or shavings of Parmesan all work wonders, as does a scattering of fresh herbs, adding flavour, colour and aroma.

Included here are several pâtés and terrines. Whether you favour chicken, fish or vegetarian, these make delicious main meals, or can be thinly sliced and served as a starter or light lunch.

ᴠ Leek and Potato Soup

This classic soup is extremely versatile. When the weather is cold, it's a wonderfully warming comfort food, but can also be served as a refreshing chilled soup on hotter days and makes an elegant starter.

⏰ **Cooking time: 6–8 hours**

👥 **Makes 2 servings**

- 25 g/1 oz/2 tbsp butter, preferably unsalted (sweet)
- 1 small onion, peeled and thinly sliced
- 1 leek, trimmed and sliced
- 1 potato, about 175 g/6 oz, peeled and cut into chunks
- 1 bay leaf

- 450 ml/³/₄ pt/2 cups hot (not boiling) vegetable stock
- 100 ml/3½ fl oz/scant ½ cup milk
- salt and white pepper

To serve
- crème fraîche (optional)

1 Melt the butter in a frying pan or saucepan, add the onion and leek and cook gently for 5 minutes until beginning to soften. Add the potato and cook for 1 minute. Transfer the vegetables to the ceramic cooking pot. Switch on the slow cooker to Auto or High.

2 Add the bay leaf and stock. Stir, then cover with the lid and cook for 1 hour. Leave on Auto or reduce the temperature to Low and cook for a further 5–7 hours until the vegetables are tender.

🌀
Cook smart
- For a chunky version, chop the onion, leek and potato into 1 cm/½ in dice and leave the soup unpuréed after cooking.

3 Discard the bay leaf. Allow the soup to cool slightly, then purée with a hand blender in the cooking pot or in a blender or food processor until smooth. Pour half the soup into a bowl or freezer container and allow to cool.

4 Stir the milk into the remaining soup and season to taste. Reheat in the slow cooker on High or in a saucepan until piping hot. Serve in warmed bowls, topped with a swirl of crème fraîche, if liked.

ⓒ **Second serving**

Either cover the cooled soup and chill in the fridge for the following day, or transfer to a freezer container and freeze for up to a month. If frozen, allow the soup to defrost in the fridge overnight. To serve, heat gently in a saucepan with 100 ml/3½ fl oz/scant ½ cup milk until hot. Alternatively, serve the soup chilled, adding a little extra milk to achieve the desired consistency as the soup will be thicker when cold.

ᕐ Main Meal Minestrone

A few staple vegetables form the basis of this soup, but you can add extras such as shredded cabbage, courgettes or celery if you have them to hand. The ready-made pesto stirred into the finished dish adds a fresh flavour and vibrant colour.

🕐 **Cooking time: 4½–6½ hours**   👥 **Makes 2 servings**

- 15 ml/1 tbsp olive oil
- 1 small onion, peeled and chopped
- 1 garlic clove, crushed
- 1 carrot, finely chopped
- 1 potato, cut into 1 cm/½ in cubes
- 400 ml/14 fl oz/1¾ cups hot (not boiling) vegetable stock
- 15 ml/1 tbsp tomato purée (paste)
- 2 tomatoes, preferably Italian plum, peeled and finely chopped
- 1 x 200 g/7 oz/small can of cannellini beans, drained and rinsed

- salt and freshly ground black pepper
- 25 g/1 oz 'quick-cook' dried spaghetti, broken into short lengths
- 10–15 ml/2–3 tsp green pesto

Optional extras

- 1 celery stick, finely chopped
- 50 g/2 oz green beans, cut into 5 cm/ 2 in lengths
- 1 courgette (zucchini), thinly sliced
- 2 savoy cabbage leaves, shredded

To serve

- crusty Italian bread

1 Heat the oil in a saucepan, add the onion and cook for 5 minutes, stirring frequently, until beginning to soften. Add the garlic, carrot and potato and cook for 1 minute.

2 Transfer the fried vegetables to the ceramic cooking pot and switch on the slow cooker to Low. Add the stock, tomato purée and tomatoes and the celery, if using. Cover the cooking pot with the lid and cook on Low for 4–6 hours.

3 Stir in the cannellini beans and the green beans and courgette, if using. Season with salt and pepper, then re-cover and cook for 1 hour.

◎ ....
Cook smart
If liked, add 2 chopped rinded rashers (slices) of smoked streaky bacon when frying the onions.
....

4 Turn up the temperature to High and allow to heat for 10 minutes. Stir in the spaghetti and the cabbage, if using. Cover and cook for a further 20 minutes or until all the vegetables and the pasta are tender.

5 Transfer half the soup to a bowl or freezer container and allow to cool. Stir the pesto into the remaining soup and serve in warmed bowls with slices of crusty Italian bread such as ciabatta.

◎ Second serving

Either cover the cooled soup and chill in the fridge for the following day, or transfer to a freezer container and freeze for up to a month. If frozen, allow the soup to defrost in the fridge overnight. To serve, transfer to a saucepan and heat until piping hot. Stir in some pesto before serving.

ʋ *Winter Lentil Soup*

Lentils contain an impressive range of nutrients including iron, zinc and B-vitamins, are rich in protein, low in fat and reputed to help fight heart disease by reducing cholesterol. They also make a very tasty soup!

🕐 **Cooking time: 6–8 hours** ⚤ **Makes 2 servings**

- 10 ml/2 tsp sunflower oil
- 1 small onion, peeled and finely chopped
- 1 celery stick, finely chopped
- 1 carrot, peeled and finely diced
- 50 g/2 oz/⅓ cup split red lentils
- 450 ml/¾ pt/2 cups hot (not boiling) vegetable stock

- 1 bay leaf
- a pinch of dried mixed herbs
- salt and freshly ground black pepper

To serve

- crusty bread or buttered toast

---

1 Heat the oil in a saucepan. Add the onion and cook for 5 minutes, then stir in the celery and carrot and cook for a further 2–3 minutes until beginning to soften.

2 Transfer the vegetables to the ceramic cooking pot. Stir in the lentils, stock, bay leaf and herbs. Cover the cooking pot with the lid and cook on Low for 6–8 hours.

3 Discard the bay leaf. Remove about 4 tablespoonfuls of the mixture and set aside. Purée the remainder in a blender or food processor until smooth. Return this to the cleaned-out cooking pot or a saucepan with the reserved mixture and stir to mix. Transfer half the soup to a bowl or freezer container and allow to cool.

4 Reheat the remaining soup until piping hot. Season to taste with salt and pepper and serve in a warmed bowl with crusty bread or hot buttered toast.

ⓒ Second serving

Either cover the cooled soup and chill in the fridge for the following day, or transfer to a freezer container and freeze for up to a month. If frozen, allow the soup to defrost in the fridge overnight. To serve, transfer to a saucepan and heat until piping hot.

🌀 Cook smart

- This soup is very similar to the dhals of Indian cooking. You can spice up the second serving if you like by stirring in 5–10 ml/1–2 tsp of your favourite curry paste before reheating, then topping the soup with a tablespoonful of thick yoghurt and serving with warm naan bread or ready-made popadoms.

- If you don't want to use celery in this recipe (you can't buy a single stick in the supermarket!) simply leave it out, or use a different vegetable such as a small parsnip or baby turnip instead. Other recipes that contain celery are Braised Lamb Shank (see page 53) and Savoury Mince (see page 48).

- If you prefer a thinner soup, stir in a little extra hot stock or milk before serving.

Spanish Chorizo Soup

A cross between a soup and a stew, this dish comes from Galicia in north-west Spain, where it is known as caldo gallego. *Every household has its own version, but it always contains chorizo, chick peas and tomatoes.*

Cooking time: 6–8 hours **Makes 2 servings**

- 1 red (bell) pepper, halved and seeded
- 5 ml/1 tsp olive oil
- 100 g/4 oz chorizo sausage, sliced and cut into small cubes
- 1 small red onion, peeled and finely chopped
- 1 garlic clove, crushed
- 1 red chilli, seeded and finely chopped
- 1 potato, peeled and cut into 1cm/½ in cubes

- ½ x 400 g/14 oz/large can of chick peas (garbanzos), drained and rinsed
- 1 x 200 g/7 oz/small can of chopped tomatoes
- 400 ml/14 fl oz/1¾ cups hot (not boiling) vegetable stock
- 1 bay leaf
- 30 ml/2 tbsp chopped fresh parsley (optional)
- salt and freshly ground black pepper

1 Remove the membranes from the pepper. Place the halves skin-side up under a preheated moderate grill (broiler) and cook for 10 minutes until the skins are slightly charred. Remove from the heat and place in a plastic bag. Leave for 10 minutes (the steam will loosen the skin), then remove and peel off the skins. Cut the pepper into 1 cm/½ in dice and place in the ceramic cooking pot.

2 Heat the oil in a saucepan, add the chorizo and cook over a moderately high heat for 2–3 minutes or until the cubes are lightly browned and the fat runs. Remove from the pan with a slotted spoon, leaving the fat behind, and add to the red pepper.

3 Turn down the heat, then add the onion, garlic and chilli to the pan. Cook for 5–6 minutes until softened, stirring frequently. Add to the ceramic cooking pot.

4 Add the potato cubes, chick peas, tomatoes, stock and bay leaf. Cover the cooking pot with the lid and cook on Low for 6–8 hours.

5 Remove the bay leaf, then stir in the parsley, if using, and season to taste with salt and pepper. Transfer half the soup to a bowl or freezer container and allow to cool. Serve the remaining soup straight away in a warmed bowl.

Second serving

Either cover the cooled soup and chill in the fridge for the following day, or transfer to a freezer container and freeze for up to a month. If frozen, allow the soup to defrost in the fridge overnight. To serve, transfer to a saucepan and heat until piping hot.

Cook smart
- Use the rest of the canned chick peas to make Vegetable Goulash (see page 93).

Goulash Soup with Dumplings

Here all the flavour of lean chuck steak is developed by gentle braising in the slow cooker until really tender. As in authentic Hungarian goulash, satisfying caraway dumplings add the finishing touch.

⏱ Cooking time: 6–7 hours **👥 Makes 2 servings**

- 15 ml/1 tbsp sunflower oil
- 225 g/8 oz lean chuck steak, cut into 2 cm/¾ in cubes
- 1 onion, peeled and sliced
- 1 garlic clove, crushed
- 1 large carrot, diced
- 5 ml/1 tsp paprika
- 1 x 200 g/7 oz/small can of chopped tomatoes
- 300 ml/½ pt/1¼ cups hot (not boiling) beef stock

- salt and freshly ground black pepper
- 75 g/3 oz green or white cabbage, finely shredded

For the caraway dumplings
- 50 g/2 oz/½ cup self-raising flour
- 25 g/1 oz/¼ cup beef or vegetable suet or grated chilled butter
- 1.5 ml/¼ tsp caraway seeds
- about 10 ml/2 tsp milk

1 Heat 10 ml/2 tsp of the oil in a frying pan, add the meat and fry until browned on all sides. Remove from the pan with a slotted spoon and transfer to the ceramic cooking pot. Switch on the slow cooker to High.

2 Add the remaining oil to the pan, then add the onion and garlic and cook over a moderate heat, stirring frequently, for 7–8 minutes until beginning to brown. Stir in the carrot. Sprinkle the paprika over and stir in, then add the tomatoes and heat until the mixture is just starting to bubble. Pour over the meat.

3 Stir in the stock and season with salt and pepper. Cover with the lid, then reduce the heat to Low and cook for 5–6 hours or until the beef and vegetables are just tender.

4 Increase the setting to High and cook the soup for a further 15 minutes, then stir in the cabbage.

5 To make the dumplings, mix the flour, a pinch of salt, the suet or butter and the caraway seeds in a bowl. Add enough milk to mix into a soft dough. Using floured hands, roll the dough into four balls. Quickly add to the casserole, re-cover and cook for 30 minutes.

6 Spoon half the soup into a warmed serving bowl and top with all the dumplings (these won't keep for another day). Serve straight away. Allow the remaining soup to cool.

◎ Second serving

Cover the cooled soup and chill in the fridge for the following day, or transfer to a freezer container and freeze for up to a month. If frozen, allow to defrost in the fridge overnight. To serve, heat in a saucepan until piping hot. A little soured (dairy sour) cream, crème fraîche or natural yoghurt makes a great finishing touch.

Mexican Bean Chowder

This is a really easy soup made mainly from storecupboard ingredients. It's up to you whether you make it really hot and spicy, as here; for a milder flavour you can reduce the amount of chilli powder or simply leave it out altogether.

Cooking time: 5–7 hours

Makes 2 servings

- 10 ml/2 tsp olive oil
- 1 red onion, finely chopped
- 1 garlic clove, crushed
- 2.5 ml/½ tsp chilli powder
- 1.5 ml/¼ tsp ground coriander (cilantro)
- 1.5 ml/¼ tsp ground cumin

- 175 ml/6 fl oz/¾ cup tomato juice
- 250 ml/8 fl oz/1 cup boiling vegetable stock
- ½ x 400 g/14 oz/large can of red kidney beans, drained
- salt and freshly ground black pepper

1 Heat the oil in a small saucepan, add the onion and cook gently for 5 minutes until beginning to soften. Stir in the garlic and spices and cook for 1 minute. Stir in a little of the tomato juice, then transfer the mixture to the ceramic cooking pot.

2 Add the remaining tomato juice, the stock and kidney beans. Cover with the lid and cook on Low for 5–7 hours until the onions are very tender.

3 Ladle about two-thirds of the soup into a blender or liquidiser and purée until smooth. Return to the slow cooker and stir well, then transfer half the soup to a bowl or freezer container and allow to cool.

4 Reheat the remaining soup on High for 20 minutes or until piping hot. Season to taste with salt and pepper and serve in a warmed bowl.

Second serving

Either cover the cooled soup and chill in the fridge for the following day, or transfer to a freezer container and freeze for up to a month. If frozen, allow the soup to defrost in the fridge overnight. To serve, transfer to a saucepan and heat until piping hot. Serve with crusty bread.

Cook smart

- If you haven't got a red onion to hand, use an ordinary white one instead.

- To make a more substantial meal, serve the soup Mexican-style by stirring in a tablespoonful of chopped fresh coriander or parsley, scattering the top with chopped avocado or a little grated Monteray Jack or mature Cheddar cheese and accompanying it with a bowl of tortilla chips.

- Use the remaining kidney beans to make Easy Chilli Beanpot (see page 80).

˅ Carrot and Coriander Soup

The slow cooker really develops and sweetens the flavour of root vegetables, so it's well worth making this soup in the slow cooker rather than on the hob. As a bonus, you can ignore it while it's cooking!

🕐 Cooking time: 6½–8½ hours | **Makes 2 servings**

- 20 g/¾ oz/1½ tbsp butter
- 1 small onion, finely chopped
- 225 g/8 oz carrots, peeled and grated
- 15 ml/1 tbsp plain (all-purpose) flour
- 450 ml/¾ pt/2 cups hot vegetable stock
- 1 bay leaf

- 15 ml/1 tbsp chopped fresh coriander (cilantro)
- salt and freshly ground black pepper
- 15–30 ml/1–2 tbsp thick yoghurt
- a sprig of fresh coriander, to garnish (optional)

1 Put the butter in the ceramic cooking pot and switch on the slow cooker to Auto or High. After 10 minutes, when the butter has melted, stir in the onion. Cover with the lid and cook for 30 minutes.

Cook smart

- This soup is also wonderful served chilled: after cooking, purée until very smooth, allow to cool, then chill in the fridge for several hours. Stir in the chopped coriander and a few spoonfuls of milk or cream before serving.

- Fingers of toasted sesame or wholemeal pitta bread make a good accompaniment.

- Carrots are often cooked with ginger and orange. To flavour with one of these, add either a knob of fresh root ginger or a finely pared strip of orange peel instead of the bay leaf. Remove at step 3.

2 Stir in the carrots, then sprinkle the flour over and stir until blended. Gradually stir in the stock, then add the bay leaf. Cover the cooking pot with the lid and reduce the temperature to Low or leave on Auto. Cook for 6–8 hours.

3 Remove the bay leaf, then stir in the chopped coriander and season to taste with salt and pepper. Transfer half the soup to a bowl or freezer container and allow to cool.

4 Serve the remaining soup in a warmed bowl, topped with yoghurt and garnished with a sprig of coriander, if liked.

ⓒ Second serving

Either cover the cooled soup and chill in the fridge for the following day, or transfer to a freezer container and freeze for up to a month. If frozen, allow the soup to defrost in the fridge overnight. To serve, transfer to a saucepan and heat until piping hot.

Lamb Mulligatawny

This is a hearty, spicy main-course soup made with chunks of lamb and thickened with rice. It's originally an Anglo-Indian dish, from the time when British cooks were discovering Indian spices! A real winter warmer and absolutely delicious.

Cooking time: 7–9 hours

Makes 2 servings

- 20 ml/4 tsp groundnut (peanut) or sunflower oil
- 225 g/8 oz lean lamb, such as fillet, neck or boneless lamb chump chops, trimmed and cut into bite-sized pieces
- 1 onion, peeled and chopped
- 1 garlic clove, crushed
- 2.5 cm/1 in piece of fresh root ginger, peeled and grated

- 5 ml/1 tsp ground cumin
- 5 ml/1 tsp ground coriander (cilantro)
- 1.5 ml/¼ tsp ground turmeric
- 600 ml/1 pt/2½ cups hot lamb or vegetable stock
- 25 g/1 oz creamed coconut, roughly chopped
- 30 ml/2 tbsp easy-cook (converted) rice
- salt and freshly ground black pepper

1 Heat 15 ml/1 tbsp of the oil in a frying pan, add the lamb and brown on all sides over a high heat. Transfer to the ceramic cooking pot with a slotted spoon, leaving behind any juices, and turn on the slow cooker to High.

2 Add the remaining oil to the frying pan. Stir in the onion and cook gently for 5 minutes until almost soft, then add the garlic, ginger, cumin, coriander and turmeric and cook for 2 minutes, stirring all the time. Stir in a little stock, then add the onion mixture to the cooking pot.

3 Add the creamed coconut to the rest of the stock and stir until dissolved. Add to the cooking pot, stir, then cover with the lid, switch the slow cooker to Low and cook for 6–8 hours or until the meat is very tender.

4 Stir the rice into the soup, cover and cook on High for a further 45 minutes until tender. Season to taste with salt and pepper. Transfer half the soup to a bowl or freezer container and allow to cool. Serve the remaining soup in a warmed bowl.

Second serving

Either cover the cooled soup and chill in the fridge for the following day, or freeze for up to a month. If frozen, allow the soup to defrost in the fridge overnight. To serve, transfer to a saucepan and heat until piping hot.

Cook smart

- Add some vegetables to the soup if you like: stir in a chopped carrot when adding the stock or, about 15 minutes before the end of the cooking time, add 50 g/2 oz thawed frozen peas.
- Some home-made or bought cucumber raita makes a good accompaniment.

French Onion Soup

One of the problems of browning onions on the hob is that they often catch and burn unless you stir them constantly. A slow cooker provides the perfect solution; the long cooking time caramelises the onions beautifully to a golden-brown.

Cooking time: 8–9 hours | Makes 2 servings

- 25 g/1 oz/2 tbsp butter, preferably unsalted (sweet)
- 5 ml/1 tsp olive oil
- 350 g/12 oz small onions, peeled and thinly sliced
- 2.5 ml/½ tsp caster (superfine) sugar
- 1 garlic clove, crushed
- 5 ml/1 tsp plain flour
- 120 ml/4 fl oz/½ cup dry white wine

- 600 ml/1 pt/2½ cups boiling vegetable stock
- 1 bay leaf
- salt and white pepper

To serve

- ½ small French stick, cut into 1cm/½ in slices
- 25 g/1 oz/¼ cup freshly grated Gruyère (Swiss) or Cheddar cheese

1 Put the butter and oil in the ceramic cooking pot and heat on High for 10–15 minutes until melted. Add the onions and stir to coat in the butter and oil. Cover the pot with the lid, then place a folded tea towel (dish cloth) on top to retain the heat. Cook for 2 hours, stirring after 1 hour. Turn to low if the onions have browned.

2 Sprinkle the sugar over the onions, add the garlic, then stir the mixture. Replace the lid and tea towel and cook on High for 3–4 hours, stirring every hour, so that the onions colour evenly; they should be dark golden and very soft at the end of cooking.

3 Sprinkle the flour over the onions and stir in. Stir in a little of the wine, then add the remaining wine, the stock and the bay leaf. Stir, then cover

again with the lid and tea towel and cook for a further 3 hours.

4 Just before serving, lightly toast the French bread slices on both sides under a moderate grill (broiler). Sprinkle one side thickly with the cheese, then grill until golden-brown and bubbling.

5 Remove the bay leaf and season the soup to taste with salt and pepper. Transfer half the soup to a bowl or freezer container and allow to cool. Serve the remaining soup in a warmed bowl with a piece of toasted cheese floating on the top and the rest served separately.

Second serving

Either cover the cooled soup and chill in the fridge for the following day, or freeze for up to a month. If frozen, allow the soup to defrost in the fridge overnight. To serve, transfer to a saucepan and heat until piping hot.

Cook smart
- It's worth making a double quantity of this soup and freezing it in individual portions.

Cheese and Lentil Pâté

Here lentils are simmered with herbs in vegetable stock, then combined with creamy goats' cheese before cooking to a lightly set pâté. This makes a great vegetarian starter, but is also good for lunch served with some crusty bread and pickles.

🕐 **Cooking time: 5 hours, plus chilling** 👥 **Makes 2 servings**

- 15 g/½ oz/1 tbsp butter, at room temperature
- 75 g/3 oz/½ cup red lentils
- 150 ml/¼ pt/⅔ cup hot (not boiling) vegetable stock
- a pinch of dried mixed herbs
- 1 bay leaf
- 50 g/2 oz soft, creamy goats' cheese
- 1 egg, lightly beaten
- salt and freshly ground black pepper
- *To serve*
- buttered toast or crackers and salad

1 Use the butter to grease the base of the cooking pot. Rinse the lentils in a sieve (strainer) under cold running water, then tip into the cooking pot. Add the stock, herbs and bay leaf. Cover with the lid and cook on High for 2 hours or until the lentils are very soft and all the stock has been absorbed.

2 Turn off the slow cooker, remove the bay leaf, then mash the lentils with a fork until fairly smooth. Leave uncovered for about 10 minutes to allow the lentils to cool slightly.

3 Meanwhile, line the bases of two 150 ml/¼ pt/⅔ cup ramekins (custard cups) with non-stick baking parchment.

4 Put the cheese in a bowl and beat briefly to soften, then gradually mix in the beaten egg. Stir in the lentil mixture and season to taste.

5 Wash the ceramic pot and return it to the slow cooker. Pour about 2.5 cm/1 in of very hot (not boiling) water into the cooking pot and switch on the slow cooker to High.

6 Divide the lentil mixture between the ramekins, smoothing the tops level, then cover each with clingfilm (plastic wrap) or foil.

7 Put the ramekins in the slow cooker and pour in enough boiling water to come half-way up the sides. Cover with the lid and cook on High for 3 hours or until the pâtés are lightly set.

8 Carefully remove from the slow cooker and place on a wire cooling rack. When cool, chill in the fridge for at least 1 hour before turning out and serving with hot buttered toast or crackers and salad.

◎ Second serving

Left in the ramekin, the pâté will keep in the fridge for up to two days, or it may be frozen, if preferred, for up to a month. If frozen, turn out and defrost in the fridge overnight or at room temperature for 3–4 hours.

Chicken Pâté

One of life's little luxuries – a rich, buttery pâté laced with alcohol. It will keep in the fridge and freezes beautifully, so it's worth making several portions at a time. Chicken livers have a very mild flavour, so season the pâté well.

Cooking time: 3 hours, plus chilling **Makes 4 servings**

- oil for greasing
- 25 g/1 oz/2 tbsp butter
- 1 shallot, finely chopped
- 225 g/8 oz chicken livers
- 1 skinless, boneless chicken breast, about 175 g/6 oz
- 15 ml/1 tbsp brandy, sherry or white wine
- 1 egg, lightly beaten
- 30 ml/2 tbsp double (heavy) cream or crème fraîche
- 2.5 ml/½ tsp dried marjoram, thyme or mixed herbs
- salt and freshly ground black pepper

To serve
- French bread or melba toast

1 Lightly oil a 600 ml/1 pt/2½ cup terrine or heatproof dish and line with non-stick baking parchment. Melt the butter in a saucepan, add the shallot and fry gently for 5 minutes until really soft. Tip into a food processor or blender and leave to cool.

2 Meanwhile, place an upturned saucer or a metal pastry (paste) cutter in the bottom of the ceramic cooking pot. Pour in about 2.5 cm/1 in of hot (not boiling) water, then turn on the slow cooker to High.

3 Roughly chop the chicken livers, removing any discoloured pieces or stringy bits. Add to the food processor. Chop the chicken breast into small pieces, then add to the food processor with the brandy, sherry or wine. Process until fairly smooth, then add the egg, cream or crème fraîche, the herbs and seasoning and process briefly again until mixed.

4 Spoon the mixture into the prepared dish and level the top. Cover with clingfilm (plastic wrap) or foil, then place in the slow cooker and pour in enough boiling water to come two-thirds of the way up the dish. Cook on High for 3 hours or until firm.

5 Carefully remove the dish from the slow cooker and place on a wire cooling rack. When cool, chill in the fridge for at least 2 hours, then turn out the pâté. Remove the lining paper and cut the pâté into eight thin or four thick slices. Serve with crusty French bread or melba toast.

Remaining servings

Wrap each portion in clingfilm or foil and either keep chilled in the fridge for up to three days or freeze for up to two months. If frozen, defrost in the fridge for 4 hours or overnight before serving.

Mixed Fish Terrine

A combination of firm white fish and pretty pink salmon gives this dish an attractive marbled effect when sliced. Even though the terrine is so simple to make, it makes a very special lunch or main course to serve on a hot summer's day.

Cooking time: 3 hours, plus chilling   Makes 2–3 servings

- 5 ml/1 tsp sunflower oil
- 150 g/5 oz smoked salmon or trout
- 400 g/14 oz skinned boneless firm white fish such as haddock, cod or whiting
- 1 egg, lightly beaten
- 60 ml/4 tbsp crème fraîche or double (heavy) cream

- 5 ml/1 tsp Dijon mustard
- 5 ml/1 tsp finely grated lemon zest (optional)
- salt and white pepper

To serve

- lemon mayonnaise or 15 ml/1 tbsp crème fraiche mixed with a little chopped fresh dill (dill weed)

1 Pour about 2.5 cm/1 in hot (not boiling) water into the ceramic cooking pot and switch on the slow cooker to High. Lightly grease a 450 ml/³/₄ pt/2 cup loaf tin or a dish with the oil.

2 Use about two-thirds of the smoked salmon or trout to line the tin or dish, allowing some of the pieces to hang over the edge. Cut the rest into strips about 5 cm/2 in long. Cut the white fish into strips of a similar length.

3 Mix together the egg, crème fraîche or cream, mustard and lemon zest, if using, in a bowl. Season with salt and pepper, then stir in the strips of fish.

4 Spoon the fish mixture into the tin or dish and smooth the surface level. Fold the overhanging pieces of salmon over the mixture. Cover tightly with clingfilm (plastic wrap) or foil.

5 Place in the cooking pot and pour in enough boiling water to come just over half-way up the sides of the tin or dish. Cover with the lid and cook on High for 3 hours or until the terrine is lightly set and a skewer inserted into the middle comes out clean.

6 Carefully remove from the slow cooker and place on a wire cooling rack. When cool, chill in the fridge for at least 2 hours before turning out and slicing. Serve with lemon mayonnaise or a sauce made from crème fraîche and chopped fresh dill.

Second serving

The terrine will keep in the fridge for a day. It's good served with a mixed salad or hot buttered new potatoes and a green vegetable.

Cook smart
- Double cream is also used in Chicken Pâté (see page 25) and Braised Pork Chop (see page 56).

Seafood

*H*ealthy and delicious, fish is eminently suitable for the slow cooker as the gentle, even cooking ensures that it retains its shape and doesn't disintegrate during cooking. Although large whole fish won't fit in the slow cooker, it's absolutely perfect for single-portion fish steaks and fillets.

Unlike meat, fish cooks relatively quickly in the slow cooker, taking about the same time as rice and pasta, so it is superb for combining with these easy-to-make all-in-one meals. Here you'll find wonderful fresh fish dishes as well as a good selection of recipes for convenient canned fish such as sardines and tuna.

Crusted Smoky Fish Pie

The potato crust, made from leftover cooked potatoes flavoured with garlic, helps to seal in all the delicious juices from the fish as it cooks. The sauce is simplicity itself, made by blending cream cheese with milk.

Cooking time: 1 hour

Makes 1 serving

- 150 g/5 oz smoked haddock fillet, skinned
- 7.5 ml/1½ tsp cornflour (cornstarch)
- salt and freshly ground black pepper
- 15 ml/1 tbsp frozen sweetcorn, thawed
- 15 ml/1 tbsp frozen peas, thawed

- 50 g/2 oz/¼ cup full-fat cream cheese
- 45 ml/3 tbsp milk

For the potato crust

- 225 g/8 oz cold cooked potatoes
- 20 g/¾ oz/1½ tbsp butter, melted
- 1 small garlic clove, crushed

1 Cut the haddock into bite-sized pieces and place in a bowl. Sprinkle the cornflour and a little salt and pepper over and toss to coat. Add the sweetcorn and peas.

2 Blend together the cream cheese and milk until smooth, then pour over the fish and vegetables (this will seem quite thick, but it will be diluted with juices from the fish as it cooks) and gently mix together. Transfer to the ceramic cooking pot and switch on to High.

3 Coarsely grate the potatoes. Mix together the butter, garlic and plenty of seasoning, then drizzle over the grated potatoes. Stir together lightly. Spoon in an even layer over the fish.

4 Cover and cook for 1 hour or until the fish is cooked. Serve hot.

Cook smart

- Any firm fish may be used for this dish, such as cod, fresh haddock or salmon. If liked, a few cooked, peeled prawns (shrimp) can be added as well.

- Brown the potato topping under a hot grill (broiler) before serving, if liked.

Coconut Salmon Steak

With its creamy and mildly spiced coconut sauce, this makes a wonderful and change from plain poached or grilled fish. If you want to make this delicious but simple dish to serve two, just double all the ingredients.

Cooking time: ¾–1 hour | **Makes 1 serving**

- 10 ml/2 tsp sunflower oil
- 1 shallot, peeled and roughly chopped
- ½ red chilli, seeded and roughly chopped
- 1 garlic clove, crushed
- 1 cm/½ in piece of fresh root ginger, grated
- 2.5 ml/½ tsp ground cumin
- 2.5 ml/½ tsp ground coriander (cilantro)

- a pinch of ground turmeric
- 25 g/1 oz creamed coconut, roughly chopped
- 150 ml/¼ pt/⅔ cup hot (not boiling) vegetable stock or water
- 150 g/5 oz salmon steak
- salt and freshly ground black pepper

To serve

- basmati rice or naan bread

1 Heat the oil in a small saucepan, add the shallot and fry gently for 5 minutes. Add the chilli, garlic and ginger and cook for 2–3 minutes or until the shallot is soft.

2 Add the cumin, coriander and turmeric and cook for 1 minute, stirring all the time, Remove the pan from the heat and stir in the coconut and stock or water. Pour the mixture into a blender or food processor and purée until smooth.

3 Pour about half the sauce into the ceramic cooking pot and switch on the slow cooker to High. Season the salmon steak with salt and pepper and add to the cooking pot. Pour the rest of the sauce over, cover with the lid and cook for ¾–1 hour or until the salmon is just cooked.

4 Carefully remove the salmon from the slow cooker and serve on a warmed plate with the sauce spooned over. Accompany the steak with steamed or boiled basmati rice or warm naan bread.

Simple Salmon Risotto

Making risotto on the hob can be tedious as you need to add the liquid bit by bit and stir constantly. In the slow cooker, it can be added all at once, then left to cook in the gentle heat with little attention.

🕐 **Cooking time: 1¾ hours**   🧍 **Makes 1 serving**

- 20 g/¾ oz/1½ tbsp butter
- 4 spring onions (scallions), trimmed and finely sliced
- 50 g/2 oz/¼ cup easy-cook (converted) Italian risotto rice
- 30 ml/2 tbsp white wine or extra stock
- 175 ml/6 fl oz/¾ cup hot (not boiling) vegetable stock

- 150 g/5 oz salmon fillet, cut into bite-size pieces
- salt and freshly ground black pepper
- 15 ml/1 tbsp chopped fresh dill (dill weed)
- freshly grated Parmesan cheese
- a sprig of fresh dill, to garnish

To serve
- French bread

1 Put the butter in the ceramic cooking pot and switch on the slow cooker to High. In about 10–15 minutes, when it has melted, stir in the spring onions, cover with the lid and cook for 30 minutes.

2 Add the rice and stir to coat in the butter, then stir in the wine, if using. Add the stock, stir, then re-cover and cook for 40 minutes, stirring once half-way through the cooking time.

3 Season the salmon pieces with salt and pepper and stir into the rice. Cook for a further 20 minutes or until the salmon is opaque and the rice is tender. Stir in the chopped dill,

then switch off the slow cooker and leave the risotto to stand for a minute.

4 Gently stir, then spoon on to a warmed plate or bowl and sprinkle with some grated Parmesan. Garnish with a sprig of fresh dill and serve at once with French bread.

Cook smart

- Strips of smoked salmon and cooked, peeled prawns (shrimp) can be used instead of fresh salmon, if preferred. Stir these in about 10 minutes before the end of the cooking time.

Mediterranean Fish Braise

Cooked with fresh herbs, fragrant orange and a dash of white wine, this is a well-flavoured fish dish that smells wonderful to come home to at the end of a long day. Serve simply with plenty of crusty French bread.

Cooking time: 1½–2½ hours **Makes 1 serving**

- 10 ml/2 tsp olive oil
- 1 small red onion, peeled and thinly sliced
- 1 garlic clove, crushed
- 2.5 ml/½ tsp fresh thyme or a small pinch of dried thyme
- a thinly pared strip of orange peel
- 1 bay leaf
- about 150 g/5 oz firm white fish fillet such as turbot, skinned

- salt and freshly ground black pepper
- 45 ml/3 tbsp fresh orange juice
- 1 firm tomato, sliced
- 4–6 stoned (pitted) black olives
- 50 ml/2 fl oz white wine

To serve

- French bread

1 Heat the oil in a saucepan, add the onion and cook gently for 5 minutes. Add the garlic and thyme and cook for 1 minute, stirring all the time.

2 Transfer the mixture to the ceramic cooking pot, add the orange peel and bay leaf and switch on the slow cooker to High.

3 Season the fish with salt and pepper, then place on top of the onion mixture. Drizzle the orange juice over, then arrange the tomato slices on top of the fish and scatter the olives around the sides.

4 Heat the wine in the saucepan to just below boiling point and slowly pour over the tomato-topped fish. Cover the slow cooker with the lid and reduce the temperature to Low.

5 Cook for 1½– 2½ hours or until the fish is opaque and flakes easily. Transfer to a warmed plate, discard the orange peel and bay leaf and serve at once with hot crusty French bread.

Cook smart

● For a more substantial dish, add a small can of artichoke hearts, drained and cut into quarters, with the olives.

● Fish or vegetable stock may be used instead of the wine, if preferred.

Easy Seafood Paella

Ready-prepared seafood can be bought in small quantities from supermarket delicatessen counters or from the chilled or freezer section, which is so useful if you're cooking for one. If you buy frozen, allow it to defrost in the fridge overnight.

🕐 **Cooking time: 2 hours**   👥 **Makes 1 serving**

- 10 ml/2 tsp olive or sunflower oil
- 1 shallot, peeled and finely chopped
- ½ red (bell) pepper, seeded and chopped
- 1 garlic clove, finely chopped
- a pinch of dried mixed herbs
- a pinch of ground turmeric
- 1 x 200 g/7 oz/small can of chopped tomatoes

- 175 ml/6 fl oz/¾ cup hot (not boiling) vegetable stock
- 75 g/3 oz/⅓ cup easy-cook (converted) rice
- salt and freshly ground black pepper
- 100 g/4 oz mixed cooked seafood (prawns, mussels and squid rings)

1 Heat the oil in a saucepan, add the shallot and cook over a medium heat for 5 minutes. Add the red pepper, garlic, herbs and turmeric and cook for 1 minute, stirring all the time.

2 Stir in the tomatoes and heat gently for a minute or two until hot, but not boiling. Transfer the mixture to the ceramic cooking pot and stir in the stock. Cover with the lid, switch on the slow cooker to High and cook for 1 hour.

3 Sprinkle the rice over the tomato mixture and season with salt and pepper. Stir, then re-cover and cook for 45 minutes.

4 Stir in the seafood, then cook for a further 10–15 minutes or until the rice is tender and most of the liquid has been absorbed. Serve at once.

Cook smart

● Fresh herbs liven up seafood dishes. If you have some to hand, stir in 15 ml/1 tbsp chopped fresh parsley or 10 ml/2 tsp chopped fresh dill (dill weed), chives or tarragon when adding the seafood.

● Red pepper is also included in Fresh Tuna with Red Pepper (see page 38) and Fish Provençal (see page 40).

Smoked Fish Kedgeree

This is a great all-in-one dish, ideal for brunch or a simple supper. Smoked haddock has been used here but, if you prefer, a flaked kipper fillet or strips of smoked salmon can be stirred into the rice towards the end of cooking instead.

Cooking time:1¼–1½ hours	Makes 1 serving
• 15 g/½ oz/1 tbsp butter	• 100 g/4 oz smoked haddock fillet, skinned
• 250 ml/8 fl oz/1 cup hot (not boiling) vegetable stock	• 15 ml/1 tbsp chopped fresh parsley, coriander (cilantro) or chives
• 75 g/3 oz/⅓ cup easy-cook (converted) rice	• 5 ml/1 tsp lemon juice
• salt and freshly ground black pepper	• 1 hard-boiled (hard-cooked) egg, quartered (optional)

1 Use the butter to grease the base of the ceramic cooking pot, then pour in the stock and switch on the slow cooker to High. Cover and allow to heat for 20 minutes.

2 Add the rice to the stock and season with salt and pepper. Stir, then re-cover and cook for 40 minutes.

3 Meanwhile, cut the fish into bite-sized pieces. Stir into the rice, then cook for a further 20 minutes or until the rice and fish are cooked and most of the liquid has been absorbed.

4 Stir in 10 ml/2 tsp of the fresh herbs and the lemon juice. Spoon the kedgeree on to a warmed plate and serve hot, garnished with the hard-boiled egg, if using, and sprinkled with the remaining chopped herbs.

Cook smart
• Take care when seasoning this dish, as smoked fish often contains salt already.

Fish Nuggets in Tomato Sauce

Providing you buy really fresh fish, these tasty nuggets can be made up to a day in advance and chilled until you are ready to cook them. Use any firm white fish; an inexpensive tail piece would be ideal.

🕐 **Cooking time: 2–2½ hours** | 👥 **Makes 1 serving**

- 1 x 200 g/7 oz/small can of chopped tomatoes
- 30 ml/2 tbsp white wine or vegetable stock
- 3–4 button mushrooms, very finely sliced
- a pinch of dried mixed herbs

- 150 g/5 oz skinned and boned white fish
- 30 ml/2 tbsp fresh white breadcrumbs
- 2 spring onions (scallions), finely chopped
- salt and freshly ground black pepper

To serve

- rice or noodles

1 Put the tomatoes, wine or stock, mushrooms and herbs in the ceramic cooking pot and switch on the slow cooker to High. Cover with the lid and cook for 1 hour.

2 Meanwhile, roughly chop the fish and put it in a food processor with the breadcrumbs and spring onions. Season generously with salt and pepper and process until the fish is finely chopped but not completely smooth. Shape the mixture into five even-sized balls and set aside.

3 Add the fish nuggets to the sauce and cook for a further 1–1½ hours or until they are thoroughly cooked and the mushrooms are tender. Serve with steamed or boiled rice or noodles.

@ **Cook smart**

- A small thinly sliced courgette (zucchini) can be used instead of the mushrooms, if preferred.

- Save time at a later date by making a double quantity of the fish balls and open-freezing (on a tray until solid) them, then packing them into a bag or freezer container. Freeze for up to a month. Separate the nuggets while still frozen and defrost on a covered plate in the fridge overnight. Make sure that you use fresh and not pre-frozen fish for this.

Braised Red Mullet

This is a great way to cook fish fillets. Red mullet is a Mediterranean fish and is at its best during the summer months. It is often cooked whole conventionally, but of course will fit better in the slow cooker if filleted.

Cooking time: 2½–2¾ hours

Makes 1 serving

- 1 fennel bulb
- 20 ml/4 tsp olive oil
- 100 ml/3½ fl oz/scant ½ cup hot (not boiling) vegetable stock
- 2 ripe tomatoes
- a sprig of fresh rosemary
- 5 ml/1 tsp balsamic vinegar
- 1 small garlic clove, crushed
- salt and freshly ground black pepper
- 1 small red mullet, about 175 g/6 oz, filleted but unskinned

1 Trim the fennel bulb, then cut it into thin slices from the top to the root end. Heat half the oil in a frying pan and cook the slices over a medium heat for 8–10 minutes, turning once, until almost tender and very lightly browned on both sides.

2 Transfer to the ceramic cooking pot and pour the stock over. Cover with the lid and switch on the slow cooker to High for a few minutes while preparing the tomatoes.

Cook smart

- The distinctive flavour of fennel goes well with other oily fish such as mackerel and trout. It would also work with white fish fillets such as plaice, dotted with a little herby butter instead of the garlicky oil and vinegar mixture.

3 Place the tomatoes in a heatproof bowl and cover with boiling water. Leave for 1 minute, then remove with a slotted spoon and peel off the skins. Quarter and seed the tomatoes, then cut into small pieces. Scatter the tomatoes over the fennel, top with the rosemary, then re-cover and cook for 2 hours.

4 Mix together the remaining oil, the vinegar, garlic and salt and pepper and lightly brush over the mullet fillet. Place skin-side down on top of the fennel mixture and cook for 30–45 minutes or until the fish is just cooked. Discard the rosemary and serve at once.

Sardine Cannelloni

This all-in-one dish makes a complete meal using a few simple ingredients, so it is great for the day before you go shopping and there's nothing much in the house. If you're really hungry, serve with some bread and a side salad as well.

Cooking time: 2–2½ hours | **Makes 1 serving**

- 20 g/³⁄₄ oz/1½ tbsp butter
- ½ small onion, very finely chopped
- 1 x 200 g/7 oz/small can of chopped tomatoes
- a pinch of dried mixed herbs
- 1 x 120 g/4½ oz/small can of sardines in oil, drained
- 25 g/1 oz/½ cup fresh white breadcrumbs
- 25 g/1 oz/3 tbsp frozen peas, thawed
- salt and freshly ground black pepper
- 5 cannelloni tubes

For the cheese sauce
- 15 g/½ oz/2 tbsp plain (all-purpose) flour
- 15 g/½ oz/1 tbsp butter
- 200 ml/7 fl oz/scant 1 cup milk
- 25 g/1 oz/¼ cup freshly grated Cheddar cheese

1 Melt 15 g/½ oz/1 tbsp of the butter in a small saucepan, add the onion and cook gently for 10 minutes until soft. Add the tomatoes and herbs and let the mixture bubble for about 5 minutes or until thick and slightly reduced. Remove from the heat.

2 Skin and bone the sardines, if preferred, then mash with a fork. Add to the tomato sauce with the breadcrumbs and peas, salt and pepper. Use the mixture to fill the cannelloni tubes.

Cook smart

- For a browned top, sprinkle a little extra grated cheese over and place under a moderate grill (broiler) until golden-brown and bubbling.

3 Grease the base and about a third of the way up the ceramic cooking pot with the remaining butter. Arrange the cannelloni tubes on the base, preferably in a single layer.

4 To make the sauce, put the flour, butter and milk in a small saucepan and cook over a medium heat, stirring all the time, until the sauce boils and thickens. Remove from the heat and stir in the cheese and a little salt and pepper.

5 Pour the sauce over the cannelloni, cover with the lid and switch on the slow cooker to Auto or High. Cook for 1 hour, then leave on Auto or reduce the temperature to Low and cook for a further 1–1½ hours or until the cannelloni is tender. Serve at once.

Thai Salmon and Rice

In this recipe a salmon fillet is briefly marinated in Thai-style spices, then steamed on a bed of rice flavoured with chilli and shallots. Serve with a fresh green vegetable such as mangetout or green beans for the perfect finishing touch.

Cooking time: 1½–1¾ hours   **Makes 1 serving**

- 15 ml/1 tbsp sunflower oil
- 2 shallots, thinly sliced
- ½ small red chilli, seeded and very finely chopped
- 250 ml/8 fl oz/1 cup hot (not boiling) mild vegetable stock
- 75 g/3 oz/⅓ cup easy-cook (converted) basmati rice
- 150 g/5 oz salmon fillet
- 15 ml/1 tbsp lime juice

- 10 ml/2 tsp Thai fish sauce
- 2.5 ml/½ tsp light muscovado or soft brown sugar
- 1 small garlic clove, finely chopped
- 15 ml/1 tbsp chopped fresh coriander (cilantro)
- 5 ml/1 tsp chopped fresh mint

To serve
- a green vegetable

1 Heat 10 ml/2 tsp of the oil in a small saucepan, add the shallots and cook gently for about 10 minutes until soft. Add the chilli and cook for 1 minute, then transfer to the ceramic cooking pot. Pour in the stock, cover with the lid and switch on the slow cooker to High for 30 minutes.

2 Stir in the rice, re-cover and cook for 15 minutes.

3 Meanwhile, place the salmon fillet on a plate. Whisk together the lime juice, Thai fish sauce, sugar and garlic and spoon over the fish. Leave to marinate for 10 minutes.

4 Stir the rice and place the fish on top. Cover again and cook for ¾–1 hour or until the fish is cooked and the rice is tender.

5 Carefully transfer the fish to a warmed plate. Stir the coriander and mint into the rice and spoon alongside the fish. Serve at once.

> **Cook smart**
>
> • Don't marinate the fish for longer than 15 minutes or it may become tough.
>
> • Lime juice has a sweeter, more subtle flavour than lemon juice, but if you don't want to buy a whole lime, use 10 ml/2 tsp bottled lemon juice instead.

Fresh Tuna with Red Pepper

Onions will caramelise to a rich golden colour if cooked slowly for a long time. A dash of balsamic vinegar enhances them and gives a wonderful sweet and sour flavour. The tuna steak is added towards the end of cooking.

🕐 Cooking time: 8 hours   👤 Makes 1 serving

- 15 g/½ oz/1 tbsp butter, preferably unsalted (sweet)
- 10 ml/2 tsp olive oil
- 1 onion, peeled and thinly sliced
- 2.5 ml/½ tsp caster (superfine) sugar
- ½ red (bell) pepper, seeded and thinly sliced
- 10 ml/2 tsp balsamic vinegar
- a pinch of dried thyme (optional)
- 150 g/5 oz tuna loin steak
- salt and freshly ground black pepper
- 30 ml/2 tbsp white wine or vegetable stock

1 Put the butter and half the oil in the ceramic cooking pot and heat on High for about 10 minutes until the butter has melted.

2 Add the onion and stir well to coat in the melted mixture. Cover with the lid, then place a folded tea towel (dish cloth) over the top to retain the heat. Cook for 3 hours, stirring every hour. Turn to low if the onions have browned.

3 Sprinkle the sugar over the onions and stir well. Replace the lid and tea towel and cook for a further 2 hours, or until soft and browned, stirring once.

4 Stir in the red pepper, vinegar and thyme, if using. Cook for 2 hours, stirring half-way through cooking. By this time the onions should be golden and the pepper slices tender.

5 Lightly brush the tuna on both sides with the remaining oil and season with salt and pepper. Spoon the wine or stock into the cooking pot, place the tuna on top of the vegetables, cover again and cook for ¾–1 hour or until the fish is tender and cooked through. Serve at once.

Cook smart

● Other firm fish such as swordfish, cod loin or sea bass can be cooked in this way.

● Double the quantity of basic onion mixture and remove half before adding the red pepper and vinegar at step 4. Use the onions as the basis for French Onion Soup (see page 23).

● Red pepper is also included in Easy Seafood Paella (see page 32) and Fish Provençal (see page 40).

Fresh Swordfish with Lentils

Puy lentils are dark green in colour and have a unique peppery flavour. They retain their shape even after long, slow cooking, which makes them perfect for this dish. You'll find them in any major supermarket.

Cooking time: 3½ hours **Makes 1 serving**

- 20 ml/4 tsp olive oil
- 1 small red onion, peeled and cut into eight wedges
- 1 fennel bulb, thinly sliced
- 1 garlic clove, crushed
- 1 small red chilli, seeded and finely chopped

- a small pinch of fennel seeds (optional)
- a small pinch of dried mixed herbs
- 50 g/2 oz/⅓ cup puy lentils, rinsed
- 250 ml/8 fl oz/1 cup hot (not boiling) vegetable stock
- 150 g/5 oz swordfish steak
- salt and freshly ground black pepper

---

1 Heat 15 ml/1 tbsp of the oil in a frying pan, add the onion and fennel and cook gently for 7–8 minutes until almost soft. Stir in the garlic, chilli, fennel seeds, if using, and herbs and cook for 1 minute.

2 Transfer the mixture to the ceramic cooking pot, stir in the lentils and stock and cover with the lid. Turn on the slow cooker to High and cook for 2½ hours or until the lentils are just tender.

3 Brush both sides of the swordfish with the remaining oil. Season the lentil mixture with salt and pepper and stir. Place the swordfish on top, re-cover and cook for 1 hour or until the fish and lentils are cooked.

Cook smart

● Double the quantity of lentil and vegetable mixture and remove half before adding the fish at step 3. Serve the following day as a salad drizzled with a little French dressing and scattered with crumbled Feta or goats' cheese.

Fish Provençal

This colourful dish contains the classic combination of tomatoes, onions, olives and peppers to give a distinct Mediterranean flavour. Serve it with slices of crusty French bread and salad for simplicity, or with potatoes and green beans.

🕐 Cooking time: 1¾ hours | **Makes 1 serving**

- 15 ml/1 tbsp olive oil
- 1 small red onion, peeled and sliced
- 1 small courgette (zucchini), sliced
- ½ yellow or red (bell) pepper, seeded and sliced
- 3 ripe tomatoes, skinned and roughly chopped
- 50 ml/2 fl oz medium-dry white wine
- 50 ml/2 fl oz hot (not boiling) vegetable stock

- a pinch of dried mixed herbs
- 150 g/5 oz firm white fish fillet
- freshly ground black pepper
- 4–6 stoned (pitted) black olives
- 5 ml/1 tsp capers in brine, drained (optional)

To serve

- crusty bread or new potatoes and green beans

1 Heat the oil in a frying pan, add the onion and fry gently for 5 minutes. Add the courgette and sliced pepper and cook for a further 2–3 minutes until almost softened. Transfer to the ceramic cooking pot and stir in the tomatoes, wine, stock and herbs. Cover with the lid and switch on the slow cooker to Auto or High. Cook for 1 hour.

2 Meanwhile, skin the fish if necessary and cut the flesh into bite-sized pieces. Season with a little black pepper. Stir the fish pieces into the vegetables and reduce the temperature to Low or leave on Auto. Cook for 30 minutes or until the fish is almost cooked and the vegetables nearly tender.

3 Stir in the olives and capers, if using. Re-cover and cook for a final 10–15 minutes to allow the fish and vegetables to finish cooking and the olives to heat through. Serve with French, Italian or rustic bread or new potatoes and green beans.

Cook smart
- Other recipes that include peppers are Easy Seafood Paella (see page 32) and Fresh Tuna with Red Pepper (see page 38).

Tuna and Pasta Bake

*A quick and easy dish and a great storecupboard standby.
Canned tuna is combined with pasta, vegetables, cream
cheese and stock and, as the pasta cooks, it soaks up the liquid
to make a deliciously creamy sauce.*

Cooking time: ¾–1 hour   **Makes 1 serving**

- 15 g/½ oz/1 tbsp butter
- 1 shallot, peeled and very finely chopped
- 50 g/2 oz button mushrooms, thinly sliced
- 1 garlic clove, crushed
- 50 g/2 oz/¼ cup cream cheese such as Mascarpone
- 200 ml/7 fl oz/scant 1 cup hot (not boiling) vegetable stock

- 50 g/2 oz dried pasta shapes
- 1 x 200 g/7 oz/small can of tuna, drained and flaked
- salt and freshly ground black pepper

To serve

- salad

1 Melt the butter in a small saucepan, add the shallot and fry gently for 5 minutes. Add the sliced mushrooms and garlic and cook for a further 3–4 minutes or until almost soft.

2 Add the cream cheese to the vegetables, then gradually blend in the stock. Turn off the heat and transfer the mixture to the ceramic cooking pot. Switch on the slow cooker on to Auto or High.

3 Add the pasta and tuna, season with salt and pepper and stir gently until thoroughly mixed. Cover with the lid and cook for ¾–1 hour until the pasta is cooked and the sauce is thick and creamy. Serve with a salad, if liked.

> **Cook smart**
> ● For a vegetarian version, omit the tuna and stir in 15 ml/1 tbsp each of thawed frozen peas and sweetcorn.

Meat

*T*he slow cooker is renowned for producing wonderful meat casseroles, stews and braises. Here, it truly excels, making even the toughest cuts meltingly tender and developing and enhancing their flavour. Included in this chapter are classic winter warmers such as Boeuf Bourguignon, Cumberland Sausage Casserole and Irish Stew, but you'll find plenty of lighter, more modern dishes as well, such as Oriental Spiced Beef and Lamb in Dill Sauce.

Nearly all the recipes make two servings to enable you to save time by either keeping half for the next day or freezing one portion for the future. Many require long, slow cooking, so you can prepare them in the morning and leave them all day to cook to perfection.

Boeuf Bourguignon

A much-loved classic from the Burgundy region of France. In this dish the beef is slowly braised in a rich red wine sauce with bacon, button onions and mushrooms. Whatever else you serve it with, don't forget a large glass of red wine!

Cooking time: 6–8 hours **Makes 2 servings**

- 50 g/2 oz button onions
- 20 ml/4 tsp olive oil
- 50 g/2 oz rindless smoked streaky bacon, cut into small pieces
- 75 g/3 oz baby button mushrooms
- 1 small garlic clove, crushed
- 120 ml/4 fl oz/½ cup hot (not boiling) beef stock
- 350 g/12 oz lean braising or chuck steak, cut into 5 cm/2 in cubes

- 5 ml/1 tsp plain (all-purpose) flour
- 100 ml/3½ fl oz/scant ½ cup red wine
- a sprig of fresh thyme or 1.5 ml/¼ tsp dried thyme
- 1 bay leaf
- salt and freshly ground black pepper
- 15 ml/1 tbsp chopped fresh parsley

To serve

- mashed potatoes and a green vegetable

1 Put the onions in a heatproof bowl and pour over enough boiling water to cover. Leave for 5 minutes.

2 Meanwhile, heat half the oil in a frying pan, add the bacon and cook until lightly browned. Transfer to the ceramic cooking pot using a slotted spoon, leaving all the fat and juices behind.

3 Drain the onions and peel off the skins when cool enough to handle. Add to the frying pan and cook gently until they begin to brown. Add the mushrooms and garlic and cook for 2 minutes, stirring. Transfer the vegetables to the cooking pot. Pour the stock over, cover with the lid and switch on the slow cooker to High.

4 Heat the remaining oil in the frying pan and fry the beef cubes until a rich dark brown on all sides. Sprinkle the flour over the meat and stir well. Gradually pour in the wine, stirring all the time, until the sauce is bubbling and thickened. Add to the cooking pot with the thyme, bay leaf and salt and pepper.

5 Reduce the heat to Low and cook for 6–8 hours or until the meat and vegetables are very tender. Remove the thyme sprig and bay leaf and stir in the parsley. Spoon half the casserole into a bowl or freezer container and allow to cool. Serve the remaining casserole at once with creamy mashed potatoes and a green vegetable.

Second serving

Either cover the cooled casserole and chill in the fridge for the following day, or transfer to a freezer container and freeze for up to a month. If frozen, allow the casserole to defrost in the fridge overnight. To serve, heat gently in a saucepan and allow to bubble for about 5 minutes.

Oriental Spiced Beef

This has all the delicious flavours of a stir-fry, but preparing it in the slow cooker allows you to use a cheaper and tastier cut of meat rather than fillet or rump steak, which can be disappointing even though it's more expensive.

Cooking time: 6–7 hours | **Makes 1 serving**

- 175 g/6 oz good-quality braising steak, such as blade
- 5 ml/1 tsp sunflower oil
- 5 ml/1 tsp sesame oil (or additional sunflower oil)
- 5ml/1 tsp finely chopped fresh root ginger
- 1 small garlic clove, crushed
- 15 ml/1 tbsp muscovado or soft dark brown sugar

- 90 ml/6 tbsp beef stock
- 30 ml/2 tbsp dry or medium-dry sherry
- 15 ml/1 tbsp soy sauce
- 50 g/2 oz button mushrooms, sliced
- 1 small carrot, peeled and cut into matchsticks

To serve
- rice or noodles

1 Trim the steak and cut it into strips. Heat the oils in a frying pan over a moderate heat, add the beef and brown on all sides. Using a slotted spoon, transfer the beef to the ceramic cooking pot, leaving any fat and juices behind.

2 Add the ginger and garlic to the pan and cook for 1 minute, stirring all the time. Turn off the heat and add the sugar, stock, sherry and soy sauce. Stir together until the sugar has dissolved, then pour the mixture over the beef (it should be hot, but not boiling) and stir.

3 Cover with the lid, switch on the slow cooker to Auto or High and cook for 1 hour.

4 Stir in the mushrooms and carrot. Leave the slow cooker on Auto or reduce the temperature to Low and cook for a further 5–6 hours until the beef and vegetables are very tender and the sauce is thick. Serve at once with boiled or steamed rice or noodles.

Cook smart
- When slicing the beef into strips, cut it across the grain, rather than with the grain, as this will make it more tender.

Beef Carbonnade

You need only a small amount of beer to enrich this casserole, so it's a good idea to choose one that you enjoy drinking as well. That way you can finish the beer when you enjoy this delicious and very satisfying meal.

Cooking time: 7–9 hours   **Makes 2 servings**

- 400 g/14 oz chuck steak, trimmed
- 15 ml/1 tbsp sunflower oil
- 1 onion, peeled and thinly sliced
- 1 garlic clove, crushed
- 5 ml/1 tsp soft brown sugar
- 10 ml/2 tsp plain (all-purpose) flour
- 120 ml/4 fl oz/½ cup light ale

- 120 ml/4 fl oz/½ cup hot (not boiling) beef stock
- 5 ml/1 tsp wine vinegar
- 1 bay leaf
- salt and freshly ground black pepper
- chopped fresh parsley, to garnish (optional)

1 Cut the meat into pieces about 5 cm/2 in square and 1 cm/½ in thick. Heat 10 ml/2 tsp of the oil in a frying pan and brown the meat on all sides. Transfer to the ceramic cooking pot with a slotted spoon, leaving the juices behind in the pan.

2 Add the remaining oil and the onion to the pan and cook gently for 5 minutes. Stir in the garlic and sugar, then sprinkle the flour over, stirring to mix. Gradually add the ale and bring to the boil. Let it bubble for a minute, then turn off the heat and stir in the stock and vinegar.

3 Pour the mixture over the beef, add the bay leaf and season with salt and pepper. Cover with the lid and switch on to Auto or High. Cook for 1 hour, then leave on Auto or reduce the heat to Low and cook for 6–8 hours or until the beef is very tender.

4 Remove the bay leaf and spoon half the casserole into a bowl or freezer container. Allow to cool. Serve the remaining casserole straight away,

garnished with a little chopped parsley, if liked.

Second serving

Either cover the cooled casserole and chill in the fridge for the following day, or transfer to a freezer container and freeze for up to a month. If frozen, allow the casserole to defrost in the fridge overnight. To serve, heat gently in a saucepan and allow to bubble for about 5 minutes.

Cook smart

● If liked, place a few baby new potatoes on top of the casserole as it cooks.

● Make a crunchy garlic bread topping for the second serving. Reheat the casserole in a heatproof casserole dish (Dutch oven), then top with 3 thin slices of French bread, lightly toasted and spread with 15 g/½ oz/1 tbsp butter blended with 1 crushed garlic clove and some salt and pepper. Cook under a moderate grill (broiler) for a few minutes until golden-brown and crisp.

Steak and Kidney Casserole

A small amount of lambs' kidney adds a subtle yet unique flavour to this classic beef dish. However, not everyone is keen on kidneys, in which case you can simply add a few extra mushrooms instead.

🕐 **Cooking time: 6–8 hours** 👥 **Makes 2 servings**

- 350 g/12 oz braising or stewing steak
- 2 lambs' kidneys
- 10 ml/2 tsp plain (all-purpose) flour
- salt and freshly ground black pepper
- 25 ml/1½ tbsp sunflower oil
- 1 small onion, peeled and chopped
- 75 g/3 oz button mushrooms, quartered

- 30 ml/2 tbsp port, red wine or extra stock
- 150 ml/¼ pt/⅔ cup hot (not boiling) beef stock
- 5 ml/1 tsp Worcestershire sauce (optional)
- a pinch of dried mixed herbs

To serve
- creamed potatoes and a green vegetable

1 Trim the meat and cut into 2 cm/ ¾ in pieces. Halve the kidneys, remove the white core, then cut them into 1 cm/½ in chunks. Mix the flour with a little salt and pepper and use this mixture to coat the beef.

2 Heat 15 ml/1 tbsp of the oil in a frying pan, add the beef and fry over a moderately high heat in two batches until browned all over. Transfer to the ceramic cooking pot with a slotted spoon and switch on the slow cooker to High. Brown the kidneys in the remaining fat in the pan and add this to the beef.

3 Heat the remaining oil in the frying pan, add the onion and cook for 5 minutes. Add the mushrooms and cook for 3–4 minutes until soft. Turn off the heat and stir in the port, red wine or extra stock.

4 Pour the onion and mushroom mixture over the meat and stir in the stock, Worcestershire sauce, if using, and herbs. Cover with the lid and reduce the temperature to Low. Cook for 6–8 hours or until the meat is very tender.

5 Spoon half the casserole into a bowl or freezer container and allow to cool. Serve the remaining casserole at once with creamed potatoes and a green vegetable such as shredded cabbage.

⊙ Second serving

Either cover the cooled casserole and chill in the fridge for the following day, or transfer to a freezer container and freeze for up to a month. If frozen, allow the casserole to defrost in the fridge overnight. To serve, heat gently in a saucepan and allow to bubble for about 5 minutes.

Meatballs in Tomato Sauce

These tasty Italian-style meatballs are great served on a bed of spaghetti or pasta. The soaked bread is a traditional touch and keeps them moist and tender. Shallots are handy to keep for singles cooking as onions can be too large.

Cooking time: 3–5 hours

Makes 2 servings

- 50 g/2 oz crustless white or wholemeal bread
- 45 ml/3 tbsp milk
- 15 ml/1 tbsp olive oil
- 1 small red onion or 2 shallots, finely sliced
- 1 garlic clove, crushed
- 2.5 ml/½ tsp ground paprika
- 1 x 400 g/14 oz/large can of chopped tomatoes
- 45 ml/3 tbsp beef stock or red wine
- 10 ml/2 tsp tomato purée (paste)
- a pinch of dried thyme
- 225 g/8 oz lean minced (ground) beef or steak
- about 10 ml/2 tsp plain (all-purpose) flour
- salt and freshly ground black pepper

To serve

- pasta and grated Parmesan cheese

1 Crumble the bread into a bowl, pour the milk over and leave to soak for about 30 minutes. Meanwhile, heat 10 ml/2 tsp of the oil in a non-stick frying pan. Add the onion or shallots and garlic and cook gently for 10 minutes or until tender.

2 Sprinkle the paprika over the onion mixture and stir in, then add the tomatoes, stock or wine, tomato purée and thyme. When the mixture is hot, but not boiling, transfer to the ceramic cooking pot, cover with the lid and switch on the slow cooker to High.

3 Add the beef to the soaked bread and season generously with salt and pepper. Mix together thoroughly, then using floured hands shape into 10 small balls.

4 Wipe the frying pan clean with kitchen paper (paper towels) and heat the remaining oil over a moderate heat. Fry the meatballs until lightly browned all over. Add to the sauce, re-cover and cook for 3 hours on High or for 1 hour on High or Auto, then 4 hours on Low, until thoroughly cooked.

5 Spoon half the meatballs and sauce into a bowl or freezer container and allow to cool. Serve the remaining meatballs and sauce with pasta and some freshly grated Parmesan, if liked.

Second serving

Either cover the cooled meatballs and chill in the fridge for the following day, or transfer to a freezer container and freeze for up to a month. If frozen, allow to defrost in the fridge overnight. To serve, heat gently in a saucepan and allow the sauce to bubble for about 5 minutes.

Savoury Mince

This basic mince mixture is incredibly versatile and can be served as a Bolognese sauce or used as the basis for a number of other dishes. The recipe given here is for two portions, but if you have a freezer it's well worth doubling the quantity.

Cooking time: 6–8 hours **Makes 2 servings**

- 225 g/8 oz lean minced (ground) beef or steak
- 1 onion, peeled and finely chopped
- 1 carrot, peeled and finely chopped
- 1 celery stick, peeled and finely chopped (optional)
- 50 g/2 oz mushrooms, chopped
- 1 garlic clove, crushed
- 1 x 200 g/7 oz/small can of chopped tomatoes

- 120 ml/4 fl oz/½ cup boiling beef stock
- 120 ml/4 fl oz/½ cup red or white wine or extra beef stock
- 5 ml/1 tsp tomato purée (paste)
- 2.5 ml/½ tsp dried oregano
- salt and freshly ground black pepper
- 15 ml/1 tbsp chopped fresh parsley, to garnish

To serve
- spaghetti and grated Parmesan cheese

1 Fry the mince in a non-stick frying pan over a moderately high heat until well-browned, stirring frequently to break up any lumps. Remove from the heat and drain through a strainer, returning the fat and juices to the pan and putting the beef in the ceramic cooking pot. Switch on the slow cooker to High.

2 Add the onion to the juices in the pan and cook for 5 minutes, stirring, until beginning to soften and colour. Add the carrot, celery, if using, mushrooms and garlic. Cook for a further 5 minutes. Add to the cooking pot with the tomatoes, stock, wine, tomato purée, oregano and salt and pepper. Stir well.

3 Cover with the lid and reduce the temperature to Low. Cook for 6–8 hours or until the meat and vegetables are very tender. Spoon half the savoury mince into a bowl or freezer container and allow to cool. Serve the remaining mince as Bolognese, spooned on to a pile of cooked spaghetti or pasta and garnish with the parsley. Sprinkle with freshly grated Parmesan, if liked.

Second serving

Either cover the cooled mince and chill in the fridge for the following day, or transfer to a freezer container and freeze for up to a month. If frozen, allow the mince to defrost in the fridge overnight. To serve, heat gently in a saucepan and allow to bubble for about 5 minutes until piping hot.

> **Cook smart**
>
> ● Other types of minced meat may be used as an alternative to beef, such as lamb, turkey or pork.
>
> ● Other recipes that include celery are Winter Lentil Soup (see page 17) and Braised Lamb Shank (see page 53).

Chilli Con Carne

Makes 2 portions

Add a seeded and finely chopped red chilli with the carrots and celery, 5 ml/1 tsp hot or mild chilli powder and 2.5 ml/^{1}/$_2$ tsp ground cumin with the tomatoes and stock. About 1 hour before the end of the cooking time, stir in half a 400 g/14 oz/large can of drained red kidney beans (use the rest of the tin to make Mexican Bean Chowder, see page 20).

Lasagne al Forno

Makes 1 portion

Use a cooled one-portion quantity of the basic mince mixture. Lightly grease the ceramic cooking pot with butter, then spoon in half the mince. Top with 1–1^1/$_2$ no-need-to pre-cook lasagne sheets, breaking them to fit. Spoon the remaining mince over and again top with lasagne. Switch on the slow cooker to High. Put 10 g/^{1}/$_3$ oz butter, 10 g/^{1}/$_3$ oz plain (all-purpose) flour and 175 ml/6 fl oz/^{3}/$_4$ cup milk in a saucepan and heat, whisking all the time, until the sauce bubbles and thickens. Stir in 25 g/1 oz/^{1}/$_4$ cup grated mature Cheddar cheese and pour over the lasagne. Sprinkle with extra grated Cheddar or freshly grated Parmesan, if liked. Cover with the lid and cook for 2 hours or until the pasta is tender.

Bobotie

Makes 1 portion

Use a cooled one-portion quantity of the basic mince mixture. Stir 15 ml/1 tbsp raisins, 5 ml/1 tsp curry powder and a pinch of ground turmeric into the mince at step 1. Spoon into the ceramic cooking pot. Cover with the lid, switch on the slow cooker to High and cook for 1 hour. Whisk together 1 egg and 120 ml/4 fl oz/^{1}/$_2$ cup milk, salt and freshly ground black pepper. Pour the egg mixture over the meat, re-cover and cook for a further ^{3}/$_4$–1 hour or until set.

Peppered Venison Steak

Venison steak is wonderfully lean, but can be slightly tough. However, it responds well to long, slow cooking and this recipe will guarantee it will be tender. If you prefer, beef braising steak makes a good alternative.

Cooking time: 5–7 hours **Makes 1 serving**

- 175 g/6 oz venison steak
- 5 ml/1 tsp plain (all-purpose) flour
- 5 ml/1 tsp Dijon mustard
- 5 ml/1 tsp black peppercorns, crushed
- freshly ground sea salt
- 10 ml/2 tsp olive oil
- 15 g/½ oz/1 tbsp butter, preferably unsalted (sweet)

- 50 g/2 oz chestnut mushrooms, sliced
- 50 ml/2 fl oz red wine
- 75 ml/3 fl oz/5 tbsp beef stock
- snipped chives, to garnish (optional)

To serve

- mashed potatoes and a green vegetable

1 Lightly dust the steak with the flour, then spread the mustard on one side. Sprinkle the mustard with the crushed peppercorns and season lightly with salt.

2 Heat the oil and butter in a frying pan over a moderately high heat until sizzling, then cook the steak on each side for about 1 minute or until browned. Transfer the steak to the ceramic cooking pot and switch on the slow cooker to High.

3 Add the mushrooms to the frying pan and cook for 2 minutes, stirring all the time. Pour in the wine and stock, then heat until piping hot, but not boiling. Pour the mixture over the steak.

4 Cover with the lid and reduce the temperature to Low. Cook for 5–7 hours or until the steak is really tender. Garnish with chives, if liked and serve with creamy mashed potatoes and a green vegetable.

Cook smart

- The red wine adds a deliciously rich flavour and deep colour to the sauce, but you can use extra stock if you prefer.

Moroccan Lamb Tagine

A tagine is a North African casserole, named after the conical earthernware cooking pot that produces a low, even heat and retains all the moisture. This recipe is a simplified version — a mixture of sweet and spicy lamb with dried fruit and almonds.

Cooking time: 6–8 hours

Makes 2 servings

- 350 g/12 oz cubed boneless lamb
- 5 ml/1 tsp ground ginger
- 5 ml/1 tsp ground turmeric
- 5 ml/1 tsp paprika
- 2.5 ml/½ tsp ground cinnamon
- 25 ml/1½ tbsp olive oil
- 1 small onion, peeled and finely chopped
- 1 garlic clove, crushed
- 150 ml/¼ pt/⅔ cup tomato juice
- 200 ml/7 fl oz/scant 1 cup hot (not boiling) lamb or vegetable stock
- 50 g/2 oz/⅓ cup no-need-to-soak dried apricots, quartered
- 25 g/1 oz sultanas (golden raisins) or seedless raisins
- salt and freshly ground pepper
- 30 ml/2 tbsp chopped fresh coriander (cilantro)
- 15 g/½ oz/2 tbsp toasted flaked (slivered) almonds, to garnish (optional)

To serve

- couscous or rice

1 Put the lamb in a bowl and sprinkle the ginger, turmeric, paprika and cinnamon over. Mix together to coat the cubes evenly in the spice mixture.

2 Heat 15 ml/1 tbsp of the oil in a frying pan. When hot, add the lamb and cook, turning frequently, until browned on all sides. Remove with a slotted spoon and place in the ceramic cooking pot. Switch on the slow cooker to Auto or High.

3 Add the remaining oil, the onion and garlic to the pan and cook for 5–6 minutes or until soft. Add the tomato juice, stirring to loosen any sediment from the frying pan, and heat gently until steaming hot, but not boiling. Pour over the meat.

4 Add the stock, dried fruit, salt and pepper, then stir briefly to mix. Cover with the lid and leave on Auto or reduce the temperature to Low. Cook for 6–8 hours or until the lamb is really tender. Stir in the coriander and adjust the seasoning if necessary.

5 Spoon half the tagine into a bowl or freezer container and allow to cool. Serve the remainder at once with the toasted almonds sprinkled over. Couscous or rice makes a good accompaniment.

Second serving

Either cover the cooled tagine and chill in the fridge for the following day, or transfer to a freezer container and freeze for up to a month. If frozen, allow to defrost in the fridge overnight. To serve, heat gently in a saucepan, bubbling for a few minutes to ensure that the tagine is piping hot.

Aromatic Lamb

Known in India as Kashmiri tamatari ghosht, this delicious dish is relatively low in fat. It already contains potatoes, so there's no need to serve it with anything else — although warm Indian-style bread makes a great accompaniment.

Cooking time: 6–8 hours | **Makes 2 servings**

- 10 ml/2 tsp sunflower oil
- 2.5 ml/½ tsp cumin seeds
- 1 small onion, peeled and thinly sliced
- 2.5 ml/½ tsp ground turmeric
- 2 whole cloves (optional)
- a pinch of ground cinnamon
- 1 bay leaf
- 350 g/12 oz lean boneless lamb, cut into chunks
- 1 garlic clove, crushed
- 2 cm/¾ in piece of fresh root ginger, grated
- 1 large potato, about 275 g/10 oz, peeled and cut into chunks
- 1 x 200 g/7 oz/small can of chopped tomatoes
- 150 ml/¼ pt/⅔ cup hot (not boiling) lamb or vegetable stock
- salt and freshly ground black pepper

To serve

- low-fat natural yoghurt and chopped fresh coriander (cilantro)

1 Heat the oil in a heavy-based frying pan and sprinkle in the cumin seeds. When they start to pop, add the onion, turmeric, cloves, if using, cinnamon and bay leaf and cook gently for 2–3 minutes.

2 Add the lamb and fry for about 10 minutes until the meat is lightly browned on all sides. Stir in the garlic and ginger and cook for 1 minute, stirring all the time. Transfer to the ceramic cooking pot and switch on the slow cooker to Low.

3 Stir in the potato, tomatoes and stock, then season with salt and pepper. Cover with the lid and cook for 6–8 hours or until the lamb and vegetables are very tender.

4 Spoon half into a bowl or freezer container and allow to cool. Serve the rest at once drizzled with yoghurt and scattered with chopped coriander.

Second serving

Either cover the cooled aromatic lamb and chill in the fridge for the following day, or transfer to a freezer container and freeze for up to a month. If frozen, allow to defrost in the fridge overnight. To serve, heat gently in a saucepan with an extra 30 ml/2 tbsp stock or water and allow it to bubble for a few minutes to ensure that it is piping hot.

Braised Lamb Shank

The perfect portion for one, lamb shanks are full of flavour and become beautifully tender when slow-cooked. They are often sold individually, too, but if they are packed in pairs, simply freeze one for another day.

Cooking time: 6–8 hours **Makes 1 serving**

- 1 large lamb shank
- a few sprigs of fresh rosemary
- 1 garlic clove, cut into slivers
- salt and freshly ground black pepper
- 15 ml/1 tbsp olive oil
- 1 small onion, peeled and finely chopped
- 1 carrot, finely diced

- 1 celery stick, finely diced (optional)
- 4 ripe tomatoes, peeled and chopped
- a pinch of dried oregano
- 75 ml/3 fl oz/5 tbsp hot (not boiling) lamb or vegetable stock
- 75 ml/3 fl oz/5 tbsp red wine or extra stock

To serve
- new potatoes and a green vegetable

1 Remove any excess fat from the lamb shank. With the tip of a sharp knife, make deep cuts all over and insert a small sprig of rosemary and a sliver of garlic into each cut. Season well with salt and pepper.

2 Heat the oil in a large frying pan, add the shank and brown on all sides. Place in the ceramic cooking pot and switch on the slow cooker to High.

3 Add the onion to the frying pan (there should be plenty of oil left; if not add a little more) and cook for 6–7 minutes, stirring frequently. Stir in the carrot, celery, if using, tomatoes and oregano. Season with salt and pepper, then add to the slow cooker.

4 Pour the stock and red wine or extra stock over and cover with the lid. Leave on Auto or reduce the temperature to Low and cook for 6–8 hours or until the meat is very tender. Serve at once with new potatoes and a green vegetable.

Cook smart
- Other recipes containing celery are Winter Lentil Soup (see page 17) and Savoury Mince (see page 48).

Irish Stew

This is a simple classic dish, made in the traditional way without any pre-cooking. It's therefore ideal if you're going to be out at work all day and don't fancy the idea of frying meat and onions before you set off.

Cooking time: 7–9 hours

Makes 2 servings

- 450 g/2 lb boned shoulder of lamb or 4 neck of lamb chops
- 1 onion, peeled and thinly sliced
- 450 g/1 lb potatoes, peeled and very thinly sliced
- 1 carrot, peeled and thinly sliced

- 1 bay leaf
- salt and freshly ground black pepper
- 300 ml/½ pt/1¼ cups hot (not boiling) lamb or vegetable stock

To serve

- peas

1 Trim off all the excess fat from the lamb. If you're using shoulder, cut it into 2.5 cm/1 in cubes.

2 Arrange the onion slices on the bottom of the ceramic cooking pot, then the potatoes, carrot and bay leaf and finally top with the meat. Season between the layers with the salt and pepper as you go.

3 Pour the stock over the meat. (If necessary, add a little more so that the meat is just covered.) Cover the slow cooker with the lid and cook on Auto or High for 1 hour.

Cook smart

- Although cooking the meat on top of the potatoes sounds unusual, it reflects the amount of time for each raw ingredient to cook. Meat takes less time than vegetables, so is placed furthest away from the heat source, which is under the base of the ceramic cooking pot.

4 Leave on Auto or reduce the temperature to Low and cook for a further 6–8 hours or until the meat and vegetables are very tender.

5 Spoon half the stew into a bowl or freezer container and allow to cool. Serve the remainder at once with some cooked peas, if liked.

Second serving

Either cover the cooled stew and chill in the fridge for the following day, or transfer to a freezer container and freeze for up to a month. If frozen, allow to defrost in the fridge overnight. To serve, heat gently in a saucepan, bubbling for a few minutes to ensure that it is piping hot.

Lamb in Dill Sauce

This recipe has a real springtime feel, with its baby new potatoes, carrots and petits pois. The dill-flavoured sauce is thickened at the end of cooking by whisking in a mixture of egg yolk and cream and sharpened with a dash of lemon juice.

🕐 **Cooking time: 5½–6½ hours**   👥 **Makes 1 serving**

- 350 g/12 oz lean boneless lamb, cut into 2.5 cm/1 in cubes
- 2 sprigs of fresh dill (dill weed)
- 1 bay leaf
- 350 ml/12 fl oz/1⅓ cups hot (not boiling) lamb stock
- 100 g/4 oz small shallots
- 10 ml/2 tsp olive oil
- 100 g/4 oz baby carrots, scraped

- 100 g/4 oz baby new potatoes, washed
- salt and white pepper
- 50 g/2 oz frozen petits pois, thawed
- 5 ml/1 tsp cornflour (cornstarch)
- 1 egg yolk
- 75 ml/3 fl oz/5 tbsp single (light) cream
- 5 ml/1 tsp lemon juice
- 30 ml/2 tbsp chopped dill

1 Put the lamb in the ceramic cooking pot with the sprigs of dill and the bay leaf. Pour the stock over, cover with the lid and switch on the slow cooker to Auto or High. Cook for 30 minutes.

2 Meanwhile, put the shallots in a heatproof bowl and pour over enough boiling water to cover. Leave for 10 minutes, then drain and peel off the skins.

3 Heat the oil in a frying pan, add the whole shallots and cook for 7–8 minutes, stirring frequently, until lightly browned.

4 Skim the surface of the lamb mixture, then remove and discard the sprigs of dill. Add the shallots, carrots, potatoes and seasoning. Leave the slow cooker on Auto or reduce the temperature to Low and cook for a further 5–6 hours, adding the petits pois 20 minutes before the end of the cooking time. Turn off the slow cooker.

5 Blend together the cornflour and egg yolk in a small bowl until smooth, then gradually mix in the cream, lemon juice and chopped dill. Stir in a few tablespoonfuls of the hot stock from the slow cooker, then return this mixture to the slow cooker in a thin stream, stirring all the time. Serve at once.

Braised Pork Chop

Dried mushrooms are an incredibly useful storecupboard standby. You might think they are rather expensive, but in fact you need to add only a few to dishes such as this to produce an incredibly intense flavour.

🕐 Cooking time: 4–6 hours	👥 Makes 1 serving

- 5 g/⅕ oz dried porcini mushrooms
- 30 ml/2 tbsp very hot water
- 10 ml/2 tsp olive oil
- 1 thick-cut pork chop, trimmed
- 30 ml/2 tbsp dry white wine or vegetable stock
- ½ x 200 g/7 oz/small can of chopped tomatoes

- 30 ml/2 tbsp double (heavy) cream
- salt and freshly ground black pepper
- 15 ml/1 tbsp chopped fresh tarragon or parsley

To serve
- buttered noodles or creamed potatoes

1 Put the mushrooms in a heatproof bowl and pour the hot water over. Leave to soak for 10 minutes.

2 Meanwhile, heat the oil in a frying pan, add the chop and brown on both sides. Transfer to the ceramic cooking pot and switch on the slow cooker to High.

3 Add the wine or stock to the pan and stir, scraping up any residue. Stir in the tomatoes and cream and heat gently until steaming hot, but not boiling. Stir in the mushrooms and their liquid, season with salt and pepper, then pour over the chop.

4 Cover with the lid and reduce the temperature to Low. Cook for 4–6 hours or until the pork is very tender. Stir the tarragon or parsley into the sauce and serve at once with buttered noodles or creamed potatoes.

Cook smart
- Double cream is also used in Mixed Fish Terrine (see page 26) and Chicken Pâté (see page 25).

Pork and Potato Hot-pot

The long, gentle cooking ensures that the pork is really tender and allows all the meat juices to be absorbed by the potatoes. This is the perfect meal for those chilly times of year when you know you'll want a good hot meal at the end of the day.

Cooking time: 6–8 hours

Makes 1 serving

- 25 g/1 oz/2 tbsp butter, softened
- 1 small onion, finely sliced
- 1 garlic clove, crushed
- a pinch of dried mixed herbs
- 225 g/8 oz potatoes, thinly sliced
- salt and freshly ground black pepper
- 200 ml/7 fl oz/scant 1 cup hot (not boiling) vegetable stock
- 1 chump or loin pork chop

1 Use about a third of the butter to lightly grease the base and slightly up the sides of the ceramic cooking pot.

2 Reserve 5 ml/1 tsp of the butter, then melt the rest in a frying pan, add the onion and cook for 7–8 minutes until softened. Stir in the garlic and cook for 1 minute. Stir in the herbs.

3 Spoon half the onion mixture into the base of the cooking pot and top with about half the potato slices. Season with salt and pepper, then pour over a little of the stock to prevent the potatoes from turning brown. Switch on the slow cooker to Auto or High.

4 Trim all the fat from the pork chop and place on the potatoes. Spoon the remaining onion mixture around the chop, then top with a final layer of potato slices. Dot the potatoes with the reserved butter. Season with a little more salt and pepper, then pour the remaining stock over.

5 Cover with the lid and cook for 1 hour, then leave on Auto, or reduce the temperature to Low and cook for 5–7 hours or until the meat and potatoes are tender.

Cook smart

- Check that the potatoes are really tender by piercing them with a fine skewer or thin knife; it should go through easily.
- If liked, the top may be dotted with a little more butter, then browned under a moderate grill (broiler) for a few minutes before serving.

Pork with Apples and Cider

Pork lends itself to fruity sauces with a touch of tartness as they help to balance the richness of the meat. Thick slices of eating apple are used for this country-style recipe as they will keep their shape better.

Cooking time: 5–7 hours | **Makes 1 serving**

- 7.5 ml/1½ tsp plain (all-purpose) flour
- salt and freshly ground black pepper
- 175 g/6 oz lean pork, trimmed and cut into cubes
- 15 ml/1 tbsp sunflower oil
- 1 small onion, peeled and cut into thin wedges
- 1 small eating (dessert) apple, e.g. Cox's, peeled, cored and cut into 8 wedges

- 100 ml/3½ fl oz/scant ½ cup medium or dry cider
- 100 ml/3½ fl oz/scant ½ cup hot (not boiling) vegetable stock
- 1 bay leaf
- 5 ml/1 tsp chopped fresh sage or a pinch of dried sage or mixed herbs

To serve

- rice or potatoes and a green vegetable

1 Season the flour with salt and pepper, then add the pork cubes and toss to coat.

2 Heat 10 ml/2 tsp of the oil in a frying pan over a moderate heat, add the pork and cook for 2–3 minutes, turning frequently, until browned on all sides. Transfer it to the ceramic cooking pot with a slotted spoon.

3 Heat the remaining oil in the pan, add the onion and fry gently for 5 minutes until almost soft. Stir in the apple, then turn off the heat. Pour in the cider and stir to loosen any sediment from the bottom of the pan. Pour the mixture over the pork.

4 Stir in the stock and herbs, then switch on the slow cooker to Auto or High. Cover with the lid and cook for 1 hour, then leave on Auto or reduce the temperature to Low and cook for 5–7 hours or until the pork is really tender. Serve at once with rice or potatoes and a green vegetable.

Cook smart
- Unsweetened apple juice can be used instead of cider, if preferred.

Apricot-stuffed Pork Fillet

Apricots have a natural affinity with pork and this simple stuffing helps to keep the meat moist as it cooks. Wrapping the fillet with Parma ham gives a luxurious touch and makes it a great dinner-party dish.

Cooking time: 4–5 hours

Makes 2 servings

- 15 g/½ oz/1 tbsp butter
- 1 shallot, finely chopped
- 5 ml/1 tsp grated orange zest
- 50 g/2 oz/¼ cup no-need-to-soak dried apricots, finely chopped
- 15 g/½ oz/¼ cup fresh white breadcrumbs
- 45 ml/3 tbsp orange juice
- salt and freshly ground black pepper

- 225–350 g/8–12 oz pork tenderloin (1 whole fillet), trimmed
- 2 slices of Parma ham
- 10 ml/2 tsp sunflower oil
- 100 ml/3½ fl oz/scant ½ cup hot (not boiling) vegetable stock

To serve

- rice or new potatoes and vegetables

1 Melt the butter in a small pan, add the shallot and fry gently for 5 minutes or until soft. Turn off the heat and stir in the orange zest, apricots, breadcrumbs, 10 ml/2 tsp of the orange juice, and salt and pepper.

2 Make a pocket in the pork fillet by cutting it lengthways, about three-quarters of the way through. Open it up and place it on a board. Cover the meat with a piece of lightly oiled baking parchment or greaseproof (waxed) paper, then gently bash with a rolling pin to flatten out the meat until it is slightly thicker than 5 mm/¼ in.

3 Spoon the apricot stuffing along the middle of the fillet, then roll it up to completely enclose the filling. Put the slices of Parma ham on the board, overlapping them slightly, so that the fat is on the outside. Place the fillet on top and roll the ham around it. Secure it in place with wooden cocktail sticks (toothpicks).

4 Cut the fillet in half widthways so that it will fit comfortably in the slow cooker. Heat the oil in a non-stick frying pan and lightly sear the fillets, then place in the ceramic cooking pot. Pour in the remaining orange juice and the stock.

5 Cover with the lid and cook on Auto or High for 1 hour, then reduce the temperature to Low and cook for a further 3–4 hours or until the meat is very tender. Turn off the slow cooker and allow the meat to rest for 10 minutes before removing and serving one of the pieces, sliced, with the sauce and accompanied by rice or new potatoes and vegetables of your choice.

Second serving

Allow the second piece of pork to cool completely, then cover and chill in the fridge for the following day. Cut into thin slices and serve with a salad.

Italian Sausage Stew

Variations of sausage and bean stew are found all over Europe. Some have lengthy ingredient lists: others are blissfully simple dishes, as here. Although spicy Italian sausages are suggested, you can use your favourite variety or plain pork sausages.

Cooking time: 6–8 hours

Makes 2 servings

- 5 ml/1 tsp olive oil
- 4 fresh spicy Italian pork sausages
- 25 g/1 oz pancetta, chopped (optional)
- 1 onion, peeled and thickly sliced
- 1 garlic clove, crushed
- ½ yellow (bell) pepper, seeded and sliced
- 1 x 400 g/14 oz/large can of chopped tomatoes

- 1 x 400 g/14 oz/large can of cannellini beans, drained and rinsed
- 45 ml/3 tbsp vegetable stock
- a pinch of dried thyme or mixed herbs
- 1 bay leaf
- salt and freshly ground black pepper

To serve

- crusty bread

1 Heat the oil in a frying pan and add the sausages and pancetta, if using. Cook over a medium heat for 6–8 minutes, turning occasionally, until lightly browned. Transfer to the ceramic cooking pot with a slotted spoon, leaving all the fat behind.

2 Drain off most of the fat, leaving just 10 ml/2 tsp in the pan. Add the onion and fry for 5 minutes, then stir in the garlic and yellow pepper and cook for 1 minute. Add to the slow cooker with the tomatoes, beans, stock, herbs and salt and pepper. Stir to combine.

3 Cover with the lid and cook on Auto or High for 1 hour, then leave on Auto or reduce the temperature to Low and cook for 5–7 hours. Remove the bay leaf, then spoon half the stew into a bowl and allow to cool. Serve the remaining stew at once with crusty bread.

Second serving

Cover the cooled stew and chill in the fridge for the following day. To serve, heat gently in a saucepan and allow to bubble for about 5 minutes to ensure it is piping hot. If liked, stir in some very finely shredded green cabbage when reheating.

Cumberland Sausage Casserole

Cumberland sausages are made to a traditional recipe and contain nothing but meat flavoured with herbs and spices. If you can't get these, you can use any sausages with a high meat content.

Cooking time: 6–8 hours **Makes 2 servings**

- 10 ml/2 tsp sunflower oil
- 275 g/10 oz Cumberland sausages, cut into bite-sized pieces
- 6 small new potatoes, scrubbed
- 1 onion, peeled and sliced
- 1 carrot, chopped
- 1 small leek, sliced
- 1 garlic clove, crushed
- 10 ml/2 tsp plain (all-purpose) flour
- 60 ml/4 tbsp red wine
- 10 ml/2 tsp tomato purée (paste)
- 150 ml/¼ pt/⅔ cup hot (not boiling) vegetable or chicken stock
- salt and freshly ground black pepper

1 Heat the oil in a frying pan, add the sausage pieces and brown for 3–4 minutes. Lift out of the pan with a slotted spoon, leaving all the fat behind, and place in the ceramic cooking pot with the potatoes.

2 Add the onion to the pan and fry gently for 5 minutes. Stir in the carrot, leek and garlic and cook for 2–3 minutes. Sprinkle the flour over and stir in, then add the red wine, a little at a time. Stir in the tomato purée, then turn off the heat.

3 Stir in the stock and season with salt and pepper. Pour over the sausage pieces, cover with the lid and switch on the slow cooker to Auto or High. Cook for 1 hour, then leave on Auto or reduce the temperature to Low and cook for a further 5–7 hours.

4 Spoon half the casserole into a bowl or freezer container and allow to cool. Serve the remaining casserole at once.

Second serving

Either cover the cooled casserole and chill in the fridge for the following day, or transfer to a freezer container and freeze for up to a month. If frozen, allow the casserole to defrost in the fridge overnight. To serve, heat gently in a saucepan and allow to bubble for about 5 minutes until thoroughly reheated.

Spicy Maple Ribs

These are the ultimate finger food. Made wonderfully tender in the slow cooker, the ribs are coated in a rich toffee-coloured sauce, so make sure you have plenty of paper napkins ready before you start eating.

Cooking time: 4–5 hours **Makes 1 serving**

- 225 g/8 oz pork spare ribs
- 1 garlic clove, crushed
- 15 ml/1 tbsp tomato ketchup (catsup)
- 15 ml/1 tbsp maple syrup
- 5 ml/1 tsp soft dark brown sugar
- 5 ml/1 tsp Dijon mustard

- 10 ml/2 tsp white or red wine vinegar
- 15 ml/1 tbsp Worcestershire sauce
- 30 ml/2 tbsp orange or apple juice

To serve
- salads and crusty rolls

1 Trim any excess fat from the ribs, then put them in the ceramic cooking pot in a single layer, if possible. Switch on the slow cooker to High or Auto.

2 Put all the remaining ingredients in a small pan and stir well. Gently heat until the mixture is just below boiling point. Pour the sauce over the ribs, turning them to coat.

3 Cover with the lid and cook for 1 hour, then leave on Auto or reduce the temperature to Low and continue to cook for a further 3–4 hours.

4 Serve the ribs on a warm platter with the sauce poured over them. They go well with cold salad dishes, such as coleslaw and potato salad, and crusty bread rolls.

Cook smart

- If you prefer a very thick sauce, pour the sauce into a pan and let it bubble over a medium-high heat until reduced by half.

- Maple-flavoured syrup isn't suitable for these sticky ribs. If you can't get pure maple syrup or don't want to buy a whole jar, substitute clear honey instead.

Chicken and poultry

Chicken is always a firm favourite. It's lean and healthy and incredibly versatile, as you'll find in this chapter.

From casseroles to curries, there's something here to suit every taste and season. Some recipes, such as Tomato and Olive Chicken, are incredibly quick and easy to prepare: others such as Chicken and Mushroom Lasagne are more time-consuming to make, but well worth the effort!

In addition, there's also delicious duck, turkey and poussin recipes to tempt you.

Pot-roast Stuffed Chicken

Tender chicken with an apricot and almond stuffing is pot-roasted here with whole new potatoes and root vegetables to make a complete meal. Perfect for Sunday lunch and while it cooks you could go to the gym or meet friends in the pub!

Cooking time: 4–5 hours   **Makes 1 serving**

- 1 chicken leg, thigh bone removed (see below)
- 15 g/½ oz/1 tbsp butter, melted
- 25 g/1 oz no-need-to-soak dried apricots, finely chopped
- 15 g/½ oz/2 tbsp toasted flaked (slivered) almonds, lightly crushed
- 15 g/½ oz/¼ cup fresh white breadcrumbs
- a pinch of dried mixed herbs
- salt and freshly ground black pepper

- 10 ml/2 tsp sunflower oil
- 5 small new potatoes, scrubbed
- 1 carrot, peeled and cut into 2.5 cm/ 1 in chunks
- 1 bay leaf
- 250 ml/8 fl oz/1 cup hot (not boiling) chicken or vegetable stock
- 5 ml/1 tsp cornflour (cornstarch)
- 5 ml/1 tsp soy sauce
- 10 ml/2 tsp red or white wine or water

1 Lightly rinse the chicken and dry with kitchen paper (paper towels). Mix together the butter, apricots, almonds, breadcrumbs and herbs and season with salt and pepper. Spoon the stuffing into the thigh cavity, fold the skin over and secure with a cocktail stick (toothpick).

2 Heat the oil in a frying pan and lightly brown the chicken on both sides. Transfer to the ceramic cooking pot and switch on the slow cooker to Auto or High.

Cook smart

● To remove the thigh bone, find the end of the bone and, with a small knife, scrape away all the meat around it until the whole bone is exposed. Finally, cut through the joint to remove the bone. (If you prefer, ask your butcher to do this for you).

3 Place the potatoes, carrot and bay leaf around the chicken portion, then pour the stock over. Cover with the lid and cook for 3–4 hours or until the chicken and vegetables are tender.

4 Blend the cornflour with the soy sauce and wine or water in a small saucepan. Transfer the chicken and vegetables to a warmed serving plate using a slotted spoon. Strain the hot cooking liquid into the saucepan, stirring. Place over a moderate heat and stir until the gravy bubbles and thickens. Season and serve with the chicken and vegetables.

Chicken Supreme

A chicken breast still on the bone with the wing attached is known as a chicken supreme. Here the flavour is enhanced by smoked bacon and juicy pear slices. You could use lardons, small cubes of bacon, instead of rashers.

🕐 **Cooking time: 3–4 hours**　　🧍 **Makes 1 serving**

- 10 ml/2 tsp sunflower oil
- 50 g/2 oz rinded smoked streaky bacon, cut into small pieces
- 4 spring onions (scallions), trimmed and sliced
- 1 skinless chicken supreme, about 150 g/5 oz
- 100 ml/3½ fl oz/scant ½ cup apple juice
- 2.5 ml/½ tsp chopped fresh thyme or a pinch of dried thyme
- 1 small firm pear, quartered, peeled, cored and thickly sliced
- salt and freshly ground black pepper
- 30 ml/2 tbsp crème fraîche (optional)

To serve
- buttered noodles or boiled rice

1 Heat half the oil in a non-stick frying pan, add the bacon and spring onions and fry until the bacon is lightly browned. Transfer to the ceramic cooking pot using a slotted spoon, leaving any fat and juices behind in the pan.

2 Heat the remaining oil and fry the chicken until lightly browned on both sides. Add to the cooking pot and switch on the slow cooker to Auto or High.

3 Pour the apple juice into the pan, add the thyme and pear slices and season with salt and pepper. Heat until steaming hot, but not boiling. Pour over the chicken.

4 Cover with the lid and cook for 2½–3 hours or until the chicken is thoroughly cooked and tender. Transfer the chicken to a warmed serving plate. Stir the crème fraîche into the sauce, if using. Spoon the sauce over the chicken, then serve at once with hot buttered noodles or boiled rice.

Chicken Chasseur

This all-time classic is usually made with chicken breasts, but in this simple version thighs have been used instead. The chicken is braised in a tomato and mushroom sauce with dry vermouth to make a healthy and hearty casserole.

Cooking time: 4–5 hours | **Makes 2 servings**

- 1 small onion, peeled and very thinly sliced
- 1 garlic clove, crushed
- 1 x 200 g/7 oz/small can of chopped tomatoes
- 75 ml/3 fl oz/5 tbsp dry vermouth
- 50 g/2 oz baby button mushrooms

- salt and freshly ground black pepper
- 1 bouquet garni or a large pinch of dried mixed herbs
- 4 skinned chicken thighs

To serve

- mashed potatoes and French (green) beans

1 Put the onion, garlic, tomatoes, vermouth and mushrooms in the ceramic cooking pot. Season generously with salt and pepper, then stir to mix together.

2 Tuck the bouquet garni under the vegetables, or stir in the dried mixed herbs, then place the chicken thighs on top, pushing them down gently to half-submerge in the liquid.

3 Cover with the lid and switch on the slow cooker to High. Cook for 4–5 hours or until the chicken and vegetables are very tender. Remove the bouquet garni.

4 Spoon half the casserole into a dish or freezer container and allow to cool. Serve the remainder at once with creamy mashed potatoes and steamed French beans.

Cook smart

- Make a bouquet garni by tying a bay leaf, a sprig of fresh thyme and a couple of parsley stalks together with string, or if preferred in a square of muslin (cheesecloth), tied at the top to make a bag.
- You can used 2 skinned chicken breasts in this recipe, if preferred.
- You could use dry white wine or stock if you don't have vermouth.

Second serving

Either cover the cooled casserole and chill in the fridge for the following day, or transfer to a freezer container and freeze for up to a month. If frozen, allow the casserole to defrost in the fridge overnight. To serve, heat gently in a saucepan, allowing it to bubble for a few minutes to ensure that it is piping hot.

Hot Southern Chicken

This chicken recipe, spiced up with chilli and cooked with a selection of vegetables and rice, is a complete meal in itself. It can be ready in less than 2 hours so it's great to set up for a weekend lunch dish. Serve it with a cold beer.

Cooking time: 1¾–2 hours   **Makes 1 serving**

- 15 ml/1 tbsp olive oil
- 15 g/½ oz/1 tbsp butter
- 1 large skinless, boneless chicken breast, cut into 3 pieces
- 1 small onion, peeled and chopped
- 1 garlic clove, peeled and finely chopped
- 1 red serrano chilli, seeded and finely chopped

- 50 g/2 oz okra (ladies' fingers) (optional)
- 1 x 200 g/7 oz/small can of chopped tomatoes
- 175 ml/6 fl oz/¾ cup hot (not boiling) chicken stock
- 75 g/3 oz/⅓ cup easy-cook (converted) rice
- 15 ml/1 tbsp frozen sweetcorn, thawed
- salt and freshly ground black pepper

1 Heat 10 ml/2 tsp of the oil and the butter in a frying pan, add the chicken and turn for 2–3 minutes until it is golden all over. Remove from the pan with a slotted spoon and place in the ceramic cooking pot. Switch on the slow cooker to High.

2 Add the remaining oil to the pan, add the onion, garlic and chilli and cook gently for 7–8 minutes until softened. Stir in the okra, if using, and the tomatoes. Heat until steaming hot, but not boiling, then add to the slow cooker. Stir in the stock, cover with the lid and cook for 1 hour.

3 Stir in the rice and sweetcorn, then season with salt and pepper. Re-cover and cook for a further ¾–1 hour or until the chicken, vegetables and rice are tender and most of the liquid has been absorbed.

Cook smart

- If you enjoy really spicy food, sprinkle in a few drops of Tabasco sauce when adding the rice.

Tomato and Olive Chicken

Chicken breast slowly cooked in stock flavoured with sun-dried tomato so that it soaks up all the lovely flavour. A few black olives add the finishing touch. This recipe is so delicious and so simple, you'll want to make it often.

Cooking time: 3–4 hours **Makes 1 serving**

- 1 boneless, skinless chicken breast, about 150 g/5 oz
- 10 ml/2 tsp plain (all-purpose) flour
- freshly ground black pepper
- 10 ml/2 tsp olive oil
- 1 bay leaf
- 1 garlic clove, peeled and finely chopped
- 10 ml/2 tsp sun-dried tomato paste
- 150 ml/¼ pt/⅔ cup hot (not boiling) chicken stock
- a few stoned (pitted) black olives

To serve
- rice and a green vegetable

1 Trim the chicken breast and pat dry on kitchen paper (paper towels). Sprinkle with a light dusting of flour and pepper. Heat the oil in a frying pan, add the chicken and cook on both sides until lightly browned.

2 Transfer the chicken to the ceramic cooking pot and tuck the bay leaf under. Switch on the slow cooker to High. Blend together the garlic, sun-dried tomato paste and stock and pour over the chicken.

3 Cover with the lid and cook for 3–4 hours or until the chicken is tender. Add the olives about 30 minutes before the end of the cooking time to allow them to heat through.

4 To serve, remove the bay leaf and accompany with steamed or boiled rice and a green vegetable.

Chicken and Mushroom Lasagne

Sheets of pasta are layered with chunks of cooked chicken and wild mushrooms and smothered with a lightly set creamy yoghurt and cheese topping to make this delicious, simple and speedy Italian-inspired dish.

Cooking time: 1¾–2 hours **Makes 1 serving**

- 15 g/½ oz/1 tbsp butter, plus extra for greasing
- 15 g/½ oz plain (all-purpose) flour
- 150 ml/¼ pt/⅔ cup milk
- 15 ml/1 tbsp olive oil
- 75 g/3 oz mixed wild mushrooms, sliced
- a pinch of dried oregano or dried mixed herbs
- 100 g/4 oz cooked chicken, cut into bite-size pieces
- salt and freshly ground black pepper
- 1 x 200 g/7 oz/small can of chopped tomatoes
- 4 sheets of no-need-to-precook lasagne
- 1 egg, lightly beaten
- 15 g/½ oz/2 tbsp finely grated Parmesan or Pecorino Romano cheese
- 150 ml/¼ pt/⅔ cup Greek-style yoghurt

1 Make a white sauce by putting the butter, flour and milk in a saucepan and bringing to the boil over a medium heat, whisking all the time, until thickened. Remove from the heat and spoon half the sauce into a bowl.

2 Heat the oil in a frying pan, add the mushrooms and fry until tender. If there is a lot of juice, turn up the heat a little and cook for a further 1–2 minutes to evaporate it. Stir the mushrooms and oregano into the white sauce in the pan and the chicken into the white sauce in the bowl. Season both with a little salt and pepper.

3 Lightly grease the base and a third of the way up the sides of the ceramic cooking pot. Spoon in half the tomatoes. Top with a sheet of lasagne, breaking it to fit if necessary. Spoon the chicken sauce over, then top with another sheet of lasagne. Spoon the remaining chopped tomatoes over, then add sheet of lasagne. Finally, spoon the mushroom sauce over and top with the last sheet of lasagne.

4 Stir together the egg, cheese and yoghurt and season with a little salt and pepper. Spoon over the top, spreading it out evenly to the edges. Cover with the lid, switch on the slow cooker to Auto or High and cook for 1 hour. Leave on Auto or reduce the temperature to Low and cook for a further ¾–1 hour or until the lasagne is tender. Serve at once.

Cook smart

● For a browned top, sprinkle with a little extra grated cheese and place under a moderate grill (broiler) until golden-brown and bubbling.

Caribbean Casserole

A true taste of the tropics; inexpensive and tasty drumsticks are cooked together with healthy brown rice and soaked dried pineapple and apricots. A scattering of toasted peanuts makes a delicious crunchy finish.

🕐 Cooking time: 3¼–4¼ hours	👤 Makes 1 serving

- 50 g/2 oz dried pineapple, chopped
- 25 g/1 oz no-need-to-soak dried apricots, chopped
- 45 ml/3 tbsp orange juice
- 2 chicken drumsticks
- 25 ml/1½ tbsp sunflower oil
- 1 small onion, peeled and chopped
- 5 ml/1 tsp mild chilli powder

- 2.5 ml/½ tsp soft brown sugar
- 250 ml/8 fl oz/1 cup hot (not boiling) chicken stock
- 75 g/3 oz/⅓ cup easy-cook (converted) brown rice
- salt and freshly ground black pepper
- 15 ml/1 tbsp chopped fresh parsley
- 25 g/1 oz/¼ cup toasted peanuts, chopped

1 Put the dried fruit in a small bowl and spoon the orange juice over. Stir, then cover and leave to soak.

2 Meanwhile, lightly rinse the chicken drumsticks and pat dry on kitchen paper (paper towels).

3 Heat 15 ml/1 tbsp of the oil in a frying pan, add the chicken and fry, turning frequently, until well-browned on all sides. Remove from the pan and arrange side by side in the ceramic cooking pot.

4 Add the remaining oil to the pan, add the onion and fry for 7–8 minutes until soft. Stir in the chilli powder and sugar and cook for 1 minute, then add to the cooking pot. Pour the stock over, cover with the lid and cook on Auto or High for 2½ hours.

5 Remove the drumsticks and stir the rice, soaked dried fruit and salt and pepper into the stock. Replace the drumsticks on top, re-cover, then cook for a further ¾–1 hour or until the chicken is well-cooked and the rice tender. Stir in the parsley and serve at once, scattered with the toasted peanuts.

@
Cook smart

- Omit the pineapple and apricot and substitute other dried tropical fruit, such as papaya (pawpaw) or mango or simply use sultanas (golden raisins) or seedless raisins.

Chicken Casserole with Juniper

This is a well-flavoured dish in which the chicken is marinated overnight in red wine, juniper berries and rosemary to give it extra flavour. You'll have to plan ahead a bit for this recipe, but it is well worth it.

Cooking time: 3–5 hours **Makes 1 serving**

- 1 chicken quarter
- 2 shallots, peeled and very thinly sliced
- 1 garlic clove, lightly crushed in its skin with the blade of a knife
- 2.5 ml/½ tsp juniper berries, lightly crushed
- 1 bay leaf
- a sprig of fresh rosemary, bruised

- 75 ml/3 fl oz/5 tbsp red wine
- 5 g/⅕ oz dried porcini mushrooms
- 60 ml/4 tbsp very hot water
- 10 ml/2 tsp olive oil
- 15 ml/1 tbsp chopped fresh parsley
- salt and freshly ground black pepper

To serve

- new or sautéed potatoes

1 Remove the skin from the chicken and place in a dish in which it fits fairly snugly. Tuck the shallots, garlic, juniper, bay leaf and rosemary around the chicken, then pour the wine over. Cover tightly and marinate in the fridge for at least 4 hours or overnight.

2 Put the mushrooms in a small bowl and spoon the hot water over. Leave to soak for 10 minutes. Remove the chicken from the marinade and pat dry on kitchen paper (paper towels). Heat the oil in a frying pan, add the chicken and cook for 3–4 minutes until lightly browned all over. Transfer to the ceramic cooking pot and switch on the slow cooker to High.

3 Pour the marinade into the pan and heat gently until steaming hot, but not boiling. Pour over the chicken. Drain the mushrooms, adding the liquid to the slow cooker. Chop the mushrooms and add them as well.

4 Cover with the lid and cook for 3–5 hours or until the chicken is very tender and thoroughly cooked.

5 Transfer the chicken to a warmed plate. Discard the bay leaf and rosemary. Stir the parsley into the sauce and season to taste with salt and pepper. Pour over the chicken and serve at once with new or sautéed potatoes.

Aromatic Chicken Curry

This is a mild, creamy curry but, if you prefer a hotter version, you could add a finely chopped seeded red chilli or 2.5 ml/ ½ tsp hot chilli powder with the spices. If you are not sure, try my version first, then spice it up next time if you wish.

Cooking time: 2–3 hours | **Makes 1 serving**

- 1 skinless, boneless chicken breast
- 25 g/1 oz creamed coconut
- 100 ml/3½ fl oz/scant ½ cup boiling chicken or vegetable stock
- 15 ml/1 tbsp sunflower oil
- 1 small onion, finely chopped
- 1 garlic clove, crushed
- 1.5 ml/¼ tsp ground turmeric

- 1.5 ml/¼ tsp ground ginger
- 2.5 ml/½ tsp ground cumin
- 5 ml/1 tsp ground coriander (cilantro)
- salt and freshly ground black pepper
- 15 ml/1 tbsp chopped fresh coriander

To serve

- rice or Indian breads

1 Trim the chicken breast, then cut into three equal-sized pieces. Roughly chop the coconut and stir it into the stock until dissolved. Set aside.

2 Heat the oil in a frying pan, add the chicken and fry briefly until lightly browned. Transfer to the ceramic cooking pot and switch on the slow cooker to High.

3 Add the onion to the frying pan and cook for 7–8 minutes until almost soft. Stir in the garlic and dry spices and cook for 1 minute, stirring all the time. Turn off the heat. Stir in a little of the coconut stock, then pour the mixture over the chicken.

4 Pour in the remaining coconut stock and season with salt and pepper. Cover with the lid and cook for 2–3 hours or until the chicken is very tender.

5 Stir in the chopped coriander and serve at once with boiled or steamed rice or warm Indian breads.

Cook smart

- Creamed coconut is sold in blocks and is a useful ingredient as it can be chopped and mixed with hot water or stock to make the required amount of coconut milk. It will keep for several months in the fridge.

Pot-roast Poussin

A whole poussin is perfect for a single serving and you can now buy them in all the major supermarkets. Here it is filled with an apple and herb stuffing, which helps flavour the meat and keeps it moist during cooking.

Cooking time: 3–4 hours

Makes 1 serving

- 25 g/1 oz/2 tbsp butter
- 2 small shallots, finely chopped
- 1 eating (dessert) apple, e.g. Cox's, cored, peeled and coarsely grated
- 15 g/½ oz/¼ cup fresh white breadcrumbs
- 5 ml/1 tsp chopped fresh thyme or 2.5 ml/½ tsp dried thyme

- salt and freshly ground black pepper
- 1 poussin (Cornish hen), about 450 g/1 lb
- 5 ml/1 tsp sunflower oil
- 60 ml/4 tbsp hot (not boiling) chicken or vegetable stock

To serve

- new potatoes or rice and a green vegetable

1 Melt half the butter in a small saucepan, add the shallots and cook gently for 5 minutes until tender. Remove from the heat and stir in the apple, breadcrumbs, thyme, salt and pepper.

2 Lightly rinse the poussin inside and out, then pat dry on kitchen paper (paper towels). Spoon the stuffing into the cavity.

3 Heat the remaining butter and the oil in a small non-stick frying pan. Add the poussin and fry until lightly browned on all sides. Place in the ceramic cooking pot and spoon the stock over. Cover with the lid and switch on the slow cooker to High.

4 Cook for 3–4 hours or until the juices run clear when the poussin is pierced through the leg joint with a fine skewer. Turn off the slow cooker and leave the poussin to rest for 10 minutes before serving with steamed new potatoes or rice and a green vegetable.

Cook smart

● If liked, serve with a whisky gravy. Tip the juices from the bottom of the cooking pot into a saucepan and skim off any excess fat. If necessary, make it up to 150 ml/¼ pt/⅔ cup with extra stock. Blend 10 ml/2 tsp cornflour (cornstarch) with 15 ml/ 1 tbsp whisky and stir into the juices. Bring to the boil and simmer for 3–4 minutes until thickened and slightly reduced. Strain into a warmed jug and serve.

Duck with Plum and Ginger

The fresh plums and spicy ginger are a wonderful combination, and the perfect foil for the rich flavour of duck. It's important to make sure that the plums you use are very ripe, or the sauce will be tart.

Cooking time: 5–6 hours | **Makes 1 serving**

- 1 duck quarter
- 1 small red onion, peeled and finely chopped
- 100 g/4 oz ripe plums, e.g. Victoria, quartered and stoned (pitted)
- 2.5 cm/1 in piece of fresh root ginger, peeled and grated

- 15 ml/1 tbsp apple or orange juice or water
- 10 ml/2 tsp redcurrant jelly
- 5 ml/1 tsp balsamic or red wine vinegar
- salt and freshly ground black pepper

1 Prick the duck skin all over with a fork to allow the fat to escape during cooking. Heat a heavy frying pan and add the duck, skin-side down. Cook for about 10 minutes or until the skin is really brown and crisp, then turn over and cook for a further 1–2 minutes. Transfer the duck to the ceramic cooking pot, leaving all the fat behind in the pan.

2 Pour away all but 10 ml/2 tsp of the duck fat, then add the onion and fry for 7–8 minutes until soft. Add the plums, ginger, fruit juice or water, redcurrant jelly and vinegar and heat gently, stirring, until the jelly has melted. Season with salt and pepper, then spoon the mixture over the duck.

3 Cover with the lid and cook on Auto or High for 1 hour, then leave on Auto or reduce to Low and cook for a further 4–5 hours or until the plums have made a thick pulpy sauce and the duck is thoroughly cooked and tender.

Duck with Pineapple Sauce

This is a delicious dish with Chinese-style vegetables. The duck fat is removed to make it not only healthier, but also so that the flavours of the sauce can penetrate the meat. Don't be put off by the list of ingredients – the recipe is really very easy.

🕐 Cooking time: 4–6 hours　　**👥 Makes 1 serving**

- 1 duck breast, about 175 g/6 oz, skinned removed
- 10 ml/2 tsp sunflower oil
- 5 ml/1 tsp balsamic or red wine vinegar
- a small pinch of ground cinnamon
- a small pinch of ground ginger
- 1 carrot, peeled and cut into matchsticks
- 4 spring onions (scallions), trimmed and thinly sliced diagonally

- 1 celery stalk, trimmed and thinly sliced diagonally (optional)
- 1 x 200 g/7 oz/small can of pineapple pieces in natural juice
- 5 ml/1 tsp hoisin sauce
- 10 ml/2 tsp light soy sauce
- 5 ml/1 tsp cornflour (cornstarch)
- freshly ground black pepper

To serve
- rice or noodles

1 Remove the skin and fat from the duck. Mix together half the oil, the vinegar and spices. Lightly brush all over the duck.

2 Heat the remaining oil in a non-stick frying pan, add the duck and cook for 1–2 minutes on each side until lightly browned. (Take care not to cook for too long, or the spices will burn). Put the duck in the ceramic cooking pot.

3 Add the carrot, spring onions and celery, if using. Drain the pineapple and add the pineapple pieces to the cooking pot. Reserve 15 ml/1 tbsp of the juice, blend the rest with the hoisin and soy sauces and pour over the duck.

4 Cover with the lid and cook on Auto or High for 1 hour. Leave on Auto or reduce the temperature to Low and continue to cook for a further 3–5 hours.

5 Remove the duck, pineapple and vegetables with a slotted spoon and transfer to a warmed serving plate. Pour the juice left in the cooking pot into a small saucepan. Blend together the cornflour and the reserved pineapple juice and stir in. Season to taste with pepper. Bring to the boil, stirring, until thickened. Pour the sauce over the duck and serve at once with rice or noodles.

Cook smart

- You probably won't need to season this dish with salt as the hoisin and soy sauces are already salty.

- Other recipes containing celery include Winter Lentil Soup (see page 17), Braised Lamb Shank (see page 53) and Savoury Mince (see page 48).

Turkey Meatballs with Rice

These tasty turkey meatballs are cooked with rice and peas in a rich tomato sauce to make a great all-in-one meal that's full of flavour but not too heavy. This recipe can also be made with minced chicken, beef or lamb.

Cooking time: 2½ hours

Makes 2 servings

- 1 x 200 g/7 oz/small can of chopped tomatoes
- 5 ml/1 tsp tomato purée (paste)
- 250 ml/8 fl oz/1 cup hot (not boiling) chicken or vegetable stock
- a pinch of dried mixed herbs
- 15 g/½ oz white or wholemeal bread, crusts removed

- 15 ml/1 tbsp milk
- 1 small garlic clove, crushed
- 175 g/6 oz minced (ground) turkey
- salt and freshly ground black pepper
- 75 g/3 oz/⅓ cup easy-cook (converted) rice
- 25 g/1 oz frozen peas, thawed

1 Put the tomatoes, tomato purée, stock and herbs in the ceramic cooking pot. Cover with the lid and switch on the slow cooker to High. Allow to heat for 30 minutes.

2 Meanwhile, break or cut the bread into very tiny pieces and place in a bowl. Mix together the milk and garlic and sprinkle over the bread. Leave to soak for 5 minutes, then add the turkey, season with salt and pepper and mix together thoroughly. Shape into 10 small balls.

3 Carefully drop the meatballs one at a time into the sauce. Re-cover and cook for 1 hour.

4 Remove the meatballs and stir the rice into the sauce. Return the meatballs and cook for a further 45 minutes.

5 Stir in the peas and cook for a final 10–15 minutes or until the meatballs are thoroughly cooked, the rice and peas tender and the sauce is thick.

6 Remove half the meatballs (but not the sauce and rice mixture as this will not reheat well) and set aside in a dish or freezer container to cool. Serve the rice and sauce and remaining meatballs at once.

Second serving

Either cover the cooled meatballs and chill in the fridge for the following day, or transfer to a freezer container and freeze for up to a month. If frozen, allow the meatballs to defrost in the fridge overnight. Reheat by gently frying in 5 ml/1 tsp oil in a non-stick pan for about 10 minutes, turning frequently, until browned and cooked through. To make a honey and mustard sauce to serve with them, add 5 ml/1 tsp honey, 10 ml/2 tsp wholegrain mustard and 75 ml/5 tbsp crème fraîche to the pan towards the end of reheating and bring to a gentle simmer. Accompany with noodles or creamy mashed potatoes and peas.

Vegetarian

*B*eing a vegetarian doesn't mean sticking to a monotonous diet or missing out on fabulous food – and not being a vegetarian doesn't mean you can't cook and enjoy these meat-free meals!

Here you'll find recipes that make use of all kinds of wonderful ingredients from beans and pulses to grains and pasta. Many are based on vegetables, which retain their shape and texture beautifully in the slow cooker.

You will find old favourites including casseroles, lasagne, chilli and ratatouille, plus plenty of more unusual recipes that are destined to become your new favourites.

Make sure that any cheeses you use are marked as being suitable for vegetarians.

Three-cheese Spinach Lasagne

Made with the classic complementary combination of Italian cheeses – Parmesan, Ricotta and Mozzarella – spinach and pine nuts, this substantial lasagne is a dish that will be enjoyed by both vegetarians and meat-eaters alike.

Cooking time: 2–2¼ hours   **Makes 1 serving**

- 25 g/1 oz/2 tbsp butter
- 20 g/¾ oz plain (all-purpose) flour
- 300 ml/½ pt/1¼ cups milk
- 1 bay leaf
- 25 g/1 oz/¼ cup freshly grated Parmesan cheese
- a pinch of freshly grated nutmeg
- salt and freshly ground black pepper

- 50 g/2 oz chopped frozen spinach, thawed and well-drained
- 75 g/3 oz/⅓ cup Ricotta cheese
- 50 g/2 oz/½ cup coarsely grated Mozzarella cheese
- 25 g/1 oz/¼ cup toasted pine nuts
- 3 sheets of no-cook-to-precook lasagne

1 Put all but 5 ml/1 tsp of the butter, the flour, milk and bay leaf in a saucepan and cook over a moderate heat, stirring all the time, until the sauce bubbles and thickens. Remove from the heat, take out the bay leaf and stir in half the Parmesan. Season with the nutmeg and salt and pepper.

2 Spoon slightly more than a third of the sauce into a bowl, cover with clingfilm (plastic wrap) and set aside. Stir the spinach and Ricotta into the remaining sauce in the pan.

> **Cook smart**
>
> ● It isn't essential to use all the different types of cheeses. You can substitute mature or medium Cheddar for both the Parmesan and Mozzarella and, if preferred, a cream cheese such as full-fat soft cream cheese or Mascarpone can be used instead of Ricotta.
>
> ● For a browned top, place under a moderate grill (broiler) until golden-brown and bubbling.

3 Lightly grease the base and sides of the ceramic cooking pot with the remaining butter. Spoon in a third of the spinach mixture, sprinkle some Mozzarella and a few pine nuts over, then top with a sheet of lasagne, breaking it to fit, if necessary. Repeat this twice more with the remaining spinach mixture, Mozzarella, pine nuts and lasagne.

4 Spread the top of the last sheet of lasagne with the reserved plain cheese sauce, then sprinkle with the rest of the Parmesan.

5 Switch on the slow cooker to Auto or High. Cover with the lid and cook for 1 hour, then leave on Auto or reduce the temperature to Low and cook for a further 1–1¼ hours or until the lasagne is tender. Serve hot.

ᴠ Vegetable and Nut Biryani

This is a lightly spiced vegetable and rice dish, and I love the crunchy texture of the nuts. I have suggested cashew nuts here because they work especially well, but unsalted roasted peanuts or pine nuts can also be used.

🕐 **Cooking time: 1½ hours**   👥 **Makes 1 serving**

- 50 g/2 oz/½ cup unsalted cashew nuts
- 15 ml/1 tbsp sunflower oil
- 75 g/3 oz cauliflower, cut into tiny florets
- 1 small onion, peeled and finely chopped
- 1 garlic clove, peeled and finely chopped
- 1 cm/½ in piece of fresh root ginger, grated
- 1 red chilli, seeded and finely chopped

- 2.5 ml/½ tsp cumin seeds or 1.5 ml/¼ tsp ground cumin
- 2.5 ml/½ tsp garam masala
- 2 whole cloves (optional)
- 250 ml/8 fl oz/1 cup hot (not boiling) vegetable stock
- 75 g/3 oz/⅓ cup easy-cook (converted) basmati rice
- 30 ml/2 tbsp frozen peas, thawed
- salt and freshly ground black pepper
- 30 ml/2 tbsp chopped fresh coriander (cilantro), to garnish

1 Dry-fry the nuts in a non-stick frying pan over a moderate heat, stirring and turning them all the time, until golden. Remove from the pan and set aside.

2 Add 5 ml/1 tsp of the oil to the pan, then fry the cauliflower florets until lightly browned and almost tender. Transfer to the ceramic cooking pot and switch on the slow cooker to High.

3 Heat the remaining oil in the pan, add the onion and cook for 7–8 minutes until soft. Stir in the garlic, ginger, chilli, cumin, garam masala and cloves, if using. Cook for 1 minute, stirring all the time. Add to the cooking pot, then pour the stock over.

4 Cover with the lid and cook for 30 minutes. Stir in the rice, re-cover and cook for 30 minutes.

5 Stir in the peas and cook for a final 15 minutes. Season with salt and pepper and serve at once, garnished with the chopped coriander and scattered with the toasted cashew nuts.

🌀 **Cook smart**

- This biryani is especially good served with bought or home-made cucumber raita or simply with a dollop of thick natural yoghurt.

Easy Chilli Beanpot

This is a great way to turn a can of baked beans into a really tasty and nutritious supper. The dumplings make it a particularly satisfying dish. If you haven't got a courgette to hand, leave it out and add a pinch of dried mixed herbs.

Cooking time: 2½ hours   **Makes 1 serving**

- 5 ml/1 tsp sunflower oil
- 1 small red onion, peeled and sliced
- 1.5 ml/¼ tsp mild chilli powder
- a pinch of ground cumin (optional)
- 5 ml/1 tsp tomato purée (paste)
- 100 ml/3½ fl oz/scant ½ cup vegetable stock
- 1 x 200 g/7 oz/small can of baked beans

- 30 ml/2 tbsp canned red kidney beans, drained and rinsed

For the dumplings
- 30 ml/2 tbsp self-raising flour
- 15 g/½ oz/2 tbsp finely grated mature Cheddar cheese
- 15 ml/1 tbsp vegetable suet or grated frozen butter
- ½ small courgette (zucchini), grated
- freshly ground black pepper

1 Heat the oil in a frying pan, add the onion and cook gently for 10 minutes until soft. Stir in the chilli powder and cumin, if using, and cook for 1 minute, stirring all the time.

2 Add the tomato purée and stock and stir over a low heat until steaming hot, but not boiling. Pour into the ceramic cooking pot and switch on the slow cooker to High. Stir in the baked beans and kidney beans, cover with the lid and cook for 2 hours.

3 Meanwhile, mix together the dumpling ingredients in a bowl. Add enough cold water to make a soft dough. Using floured hands, shape into three equal-sized balls and gently place on top of the beans. Re-cover and cook for a further 30 minutes or until the dumplings are well risen.

4 Serve the bean hot-pot at once.

Cook smart

● Add the dumplings quickly to the slow cooker so that little heat is lost, and do not lift the lid to check them while cooking or they may sink.

● If you're really hungry, a poached or fried egg or a sprinkling of grated Cheddar cheese will make the meal more substantial.

● Use the rest of the kidney beans to make Mexican Bean Chowder (see page 20).

Cheese Fondue

Fondue is usually made with a mixture of cheeses, but is still good if you only want to buy one type. Traditionally, the cheese is melted in an earthernware pot on the hob; the slow cooker does the job just as well.

Cooking time: 1½ hours   **Makes 1 serving**

- 5 ml/1 tsp unsalted (sweet) butter
- 1 small whole garlic clove, peeled
- 60 ml/4 tbsp dry white wine, cider or light ale
- 75 g/3 oz/¾ cup freshly grated Gruyère (Swiss) cheese, or half Gruyère and half Emmental cheese
- 2.5 ml/½ tsp cornflour (cornstarch)
- 15 ml/1 tbsp kirsch
- a pinch of freshly grated nutmeg
- salt and white pepper

To serve

- ½ small baguette, cut into cubes and/or vegetable crudités and pretzels

1 Grease the base of the ceramic cooking pot with the butter, then rub the base and sides with the garlic clove. Pour in the wine, cider or ale, cover and switch on the slow cooker to High.

2 After 30 minutes, add the cheese, then re-cover. Cook for 1 hour, stirring once or twice, until the cheese has melted and the mixture is smooth.

3 Blend together the cornflour and kirsch and stir into the mixture with the nutmeg and some salt and pepper.

4 Reduce the temperature to Low to keep the fondue warm. Serve with a selection of cubes of bread, vegetables crudités and pretzels on long forks for dipping.

Cook smart

- This makes a great quick meal for one – or double up the quantities for sharing.

- Bread that is one or two days old is ideal as it is firm and won't go soggy when coated with the fondue. Push the bread on to your fork with the crumb edge first and it will be less likely to fall off when dipped.

- You can use extra wine, cider or ale if you haven't any kirsch.

Lentil and Vegetable Casserole

Here's an easy vegetarian dish that makes a satisfying main course all on its own. It's similar to the delicious spicy dhals from India, but is packed with chunky potatoes, carrots and parsnip, giving it a wonderful texture.

Cooking time: 5–7 hours

Makes 2 servings

- 350 g/12 oz new potatoes, scrubbed
- 10 ml/2 tsp sunflower oil
- 1 small onion, peeled and chopped
- 1 garlic clove, crushed
- 15 ml/1 tbsp curry paste or powder
- 400 ml/14 fl oz/1¾ cups hot (not boiling) vegetable stock
- 2 carrots, thickly sliced

- 1 parsnip, thickly sliced
- 50 g/2 oz/⅓ cup red lentils
- salt and freshly ground black pepper
- 30 ml/2 tbsp chopped fresh coriander (cilantro)

To serve
- thick natural yoghurt and naan bread

1 Halve the potatoes or cut them into 2.5cm/1 in chunks to make the pieces equally sized.

2 Heat the oil in a frying pan, add the onion and cook for 5 minutes. Add the garlic and cook for 2–3 minutes until softened. Stir in the curry paste or powder and cook for 1 minute, stirring all the time.

3 Turn off the heat. Stir in a little of the stock, then transfer the mixture to the ceramic cooking pot. Add the potatoes, carrots, parsnip, lentils and the remaining stock, then season with salt and pepper. Stir to combine, then cover with the lid and switch on the slow cooker to Auto or High.

4 Cook for 1 hour, then leave on Auto or reduce the temperature to Low and cook for 4–6 hours or until the vegetables and lentils are very tender.

5 Stir in the coriander, then taste and adjust the seasoning if necessary. Spoon half the casserole into a dish and leave to cool. Serve the remaining casserole at once, drizzled with a little yoghurt and naan bread, if liked.

Second serving

Cover the cooled casserole and chill in the fridge for the following day. To serve, heat gently in a saucepan with a little extra stock or water until bubbling and hot.

Cook smart

● Other vegetables, such as butternut squash, swede (rutabaga) or celeriac (celery root) may be used in this dish. These are often sold whole, but can occasionally be found in small portions in 'casserole packs' in the vegetables section.

Puy Lentil Vegetable Casserole

Unlike other lentils, tiny olive-green puy lentils retain their shape even after long, slow cooking, so this casserole is ideal for all-day cooking. They are also full of goodness and taste great cooked in this way.

Cooking time: 6–8 hours

Makes 2 servings

- 10 ml/2 tsp sunflower oil
- 1 small red onion, peeled and cut into thin wedges
- 1 garlic clove, peeled and finely chopped
- 1 red chilli, seeded and chopped
- 1 acorn squash, peeled, seeded and sliced
- 1 small fennel bulb, trimmed and sliced

- 75 g/3 oz/½ cup puy lentils, rinsed
- 375 ml/13 fl oz/1½ cups hot (not boiling) vegetable stock
- a pinch of dried mixed herbs
- salt and freshly ground black pepper

To serve

- crumbled Feta or goats' cheese and soda bread

1 Heat the oil in a frying pan, add the onion, garlic and chilli and cook gently for 5 minutes until beginning to soften. Transfer to the ceramic cooking pot and add all the remaining ingredients.

2 Stir well, then cover with the lid and cook on Low for 6–8 hours or until the both the lentils and the vegetables are tender and most of the stock has been absorbed.

3 Spoon half the casserole into a bowl or freezer container and allow to cool. Serve the remainder at once, scattered with crumbled Feta or goats' cheese. Soda bread also makes a good accompaniment.

Second serving

Either cover the cooled casserole and chill in the fridge for the following day, or transfer to a freezer container and freeze for up to a month. If frozen, allow the casserole to defrost in the fridge overnight. To serve, heat gently in a saucepan with an extra tablespoonful or two of stock. Let it bubble for a few minutes to ensure it is piping hot. Serve sprinkled with a few toasted almonds, if liked.

Cook smart

● Choose a small acorn squash, about 450g/1 lb in weight before preparation. Alternatively, you can use a wedge of pumpkin or another variety of squash.

✎ Bean Chilli with Cornbread

Here red kidney beans are simmered in a mildly spiced tomato sauce until they have absorbed all the wonderful flavours, and are then topped with a light cornmeal crust. It's essential that dried kidney beans are boiled rapidly before being added.

🕐 Cooking time: 7–9 hours + soaking 👥 Makes 2 servings

- 100 g/4 oz/1 cup dried red kidney beans
- 1 bay leaf
- 10 ml/2 tsp olive oil
- 1 small onion, peeled and finely chopped
- 1 garlic clove, crushed
- 1 celery stick, sliced
- 2.5 ml/½ tsp ground chilli
- 2.5 ml/½ tsp ground cumin
- 1.5 ml/¼ tsp dried mixed herbs
- 1 x 200 g/7 oz/small can of chopped tomatoes
- 5 ml/1 tsp tomato purée (paste)
- salt and freshly ground black pepper

For the cornbread topping
- 75 g/3 oz/¾ cup cornmeal
- 10 ml/2 tsp wholemeal or plain (all-purpose) flour
- 2.5 ml/½ tsp baking powder
- 1 egg, lightly beaten
- 50 ml/2 fl oz milk

To serve
- a green vegetable

1 Put the kidney beans in a bowl and pour over plenty of cold water. Leave them to soak for at least 6 hours or overnight. Drain and rinse, then put in a saucepan with 400 ml/14 fl oz/ 1¾ cups cold water. Bring to the boil, then boil rapidly uncovered for 10 minutes. Turn off the heat and leave to cool for a few minutes.

2 Tip the beans and their liquid into the ceramic cooking pot. Add the bay leaf. Cover with the lid and switch on the slow cooker to Auto or High.

3 Heat the oil in a frying pan, add the onion and cook for 5 minutes. Add the garlic and celery and cook for 3–4 minutes until fairly soft. Stir in the chilli, cumin and herbs and cook for a few seconds more, then add the mixture to the cooking pot.

4 Cover and cook for 1 hour, then leave on Auto or reduce the temperature to Low and cook for a further 6–8 hours or until the beans are very tender.

5 Remove the bay leaf, then stir in the tomatoes, tomato purée and salt and pepper. Increase the temperature to High and cook for 20 minutes.

6 Meanwhile, to make the topping, put the cornmeal, flour, baking powder and a pinch of salt in a bowl and stir together. Make a well in the middle, add the egg and milk and mix to a stiff batter. Spoon over the bean mixture and cook for a further 40 minutes or until the topping is well-risen and firm.

7 Spoon half the bean chilli and topping into a heatproof dish and leave to cool. Serve the rest at once with a freshly cooked green vegetable.

Second serving

Cover the cooled bean chilli and chill in the fridge for the following day. Reheat, covered with foil in a moderate oven, or covered in clingfilm (plastic wrap) in the microwave, until hot.

Cook smart

● Raw red kidney beans contain toxins which are destroyed by the rapid boiling for 10 minutes at step 1.

● Other recipes that include celery are Winter Lentil Soup (see page 17), Butter Bean Bake (see page 86), Braised Lamb Shank (see page 53) and Savoury Mince (see page 48).

Butter Bean Bake

This dish is cooked in a loaf tin or round dish, and is sliced to serve as you would a pâté. It is delicious hot with a selection of vegetables, but is equally good cold with a fresh salad. A very easy and versatile recipe not just for vegetarians.

Cooking time: 3 hours   **Makes 2 servings**

- 1 x 425 g/15 oz/large can of butter (lima) beans, drained and rinsed
- 30 ml/2 tbsp milk
- 4 spring onions (scallions), trimmed and sliced
- 1 celery stick, chopped
- 25 g/1 oz/½ cup fresh white breadcrumbs

- 30 ml/2 tbsp chopped fresh parsley
- 1 egg, lightly beaten
- 75 g/3 oz/¾ cup freshly grated Cheddar cheese
- salt and freshly ground black pepper
- oil or butter for greasing

To serve

- vegetables of your choice or salad

1 Place an upturned saucer or a metal pastry (paste) cutter in the bottom of the ceramic cooking pot. Pour in about 2.5 cm/1 in hot (not boiling) water and switch on the slow cooker to High.

2 Put the butter beans, milk, spring onions and celery in a food processor and blend until fairly smooth. Transfer the mixture to a bowl, then add all the remaining ingredients and mix thoroughly. Spoon into a greased and lined 450 g/1 lb loaf tin or soufflé dish, level the top and cover with clingfilm (plastic wrap).

3 Place in the slow cooker and pour in enough boiling water to come two-thirds of the way up the sides of the tin or dish. Cover with the lid and cook for 3 hours or until firm and a skewer inserted into the middle comes out hot.

4 Carefully remove from the slow cooker and place on a wire cooling rack. Leave for 5 minutes before turning out. If serving hot, cut off two thick slices and serve at once with fresh vegetables. If serving cold, leave to cool completely and chill before slicing.

Second serving

Wrap the remaining butter bean bake in clingfilm and keep in the fridge for up to 2 days.

Cook smart

- Other canned beans may be substituted for the butter beans, if preferred.
- Other recipes that include celery are Winter Lentil Soup (see page 17), Braised Lamb Shank (see page 53), Savoury Mince (see page 48) and Bean Chilli with Cornbread (see page 84).

Egg-topped Ratatouille

This is a tasty way to ensure that you're eating a wide variety and plenty of fresh vegetables. Served with an egg it makes a high-protein vegetarian dish, but would also be wonderful as a vegetable dish in its own right.

Cooking time: 4¼–6¼ hours **Makes 2 servings**

- 225 g/8 oz ripe plum tomatoes, chopped
- 75 ml/3 fl oz/5 tbsp hot (not boiling) vegetable stock
- 15 ml/1 tbsp olive oil
- 1 small red onion, peeled and chopped
- 1 garlic clove, peeled and finely chopped
- 1 small aubergine (eggplant), trimmed and cut into 1 cm/½ in dice
- 1 small yellow or red (bell) pepper, quartered, seeded and sliced
- 1 courgette (zucchini), trimmed and sliced
- salt and freshly ground black pepper
- 1 egg
- 15 ml/1 tbsp torn fresh basil leaves
- freshly shaved Parmesan cheese

To serve
- crusty bread

1 Put the tomatoes and stock in the ceramic cooking pot, cover with a lid and switch on the slow cooker to High.

2 Heat the oil in a frying pan, add the onion and cook for 7–8 minutes until soft. Add the garlic and cook for 1 minute. Add to the cooking pot with all the remaining vegetables. Season with salt and pepper, mix well, then re-cover and cook for 4–6 hours or until the vegetables are tender. If possible, stir the mixture half-way through the cooking time.

3 Stir the ratatouille mixture and make a small hollow in the middle. Break the egg on to a saucer, then gently tip into the hollow. Re-cover and cook for a further 15 minutes or until the egg white is set and the yolk is still soft, or a little longer if you prefer the egg firmer.

4 Carefully spoon half the ratatouille mixture and the egg on to a warmed serving plate. Scatter with the basil and Parmesan shavings and serve at once with warm crusty bread.

Second serving

Transfer the remaining ratatouille to a bowl and leave to cool, then cover and chill in the fridge for the following day. Reheat in a saucepan with an extra tablespoonful of stock until hot and bubbling. Serve scattered with plenty of grated or crumbled cheese and crusty bread.

Cook smart
- Some vegetables cook more quickly than others in the slow cooker and the courgette will be very soft by the end of the cooking time. If you prefer a firmer texture, add it to the cooking pot 2 hours after the other vegetables.

Bulghar Risotto

Also known as cracked wheat, burghul and pourgouri,
bulghar is made by coarsely grinding wheat grains, then
parboiling them, so it's easy and relatively quick to prepare.
It's a useful standby for both hot dishes and cold salads.

Cooking time: 30 minutes   **Makes 2 servings**

- 100 g/4 oz/1 cup bulghar (cracked wheat)
- 350 ml/12 fl oz/1⅓ cups hot (not boiling) vegetable stock
- 15 ml/1 tbsp olive oil
- 2 small courgettes (zucchini), trimmed and thinly sliced
- 4 spring onions (scallions), trimmed and diagonally sliced
- 1 garlic clove, crushed

- 1 carrot, peeled and coarsely grated
- salt and freshly ground black pepper
- 4 no-need-to-soak dried apricots, chopped
- 40 g/1½ oz/¼ cup raisins
- juice of ½ lemon
- 15 ml/1 tbsp chopped fresh mint or parsley (optional)
- a sprig of mint or parsley, to garnish

1 Put the bulghar in the ceramic cooking pot and pour the stock over. Switch on the slow cooker to High and cover with the lid.

2 Heat the oil in a frying pan, add the courgette and cook gently for 3–4 minutes. Add the spring onions and cook for 2–3 minutes or the onions and courgette are almost tender. Turn off the heat and stir in the garlic, carrot and salt and pepper.

3 Stir the vegetables into the bulghar, cover with the lid and cook on high for 30 minutes or until the bulghar is tender and all the stock has been absorbed.

4 Meanwhile, put the apricots and raisins in a small bowl with the lemon juice and leave to soak.

5 Turn off the slow cooker and stir in the soaked apricots and raisins and the mint or parsley, if using. Re-cover and leave to stand for 5 minutes. Spoon half the risotto into a bowl and allow to cool. Serve the rest hot, garnished with a sprig of mint or parsley.

Second serving

Cover the cooled risotto and chill in the fridge for the following day. Serve it as a salad with some goats' or blue cheese crumbled over.

Cook smart
- For a spicier dish, soak a pinch of crushed dried chillies with the fruit.

Vegetable Crumble

Crumbles don't have to be sweet. This colourful one-pot savoury version with its oat, nut and cheese topping is ideal for a mid-week meal. Sweet potatoes are readily available in major supermarkets as well as ethnic food stores.

Cooking time: 6–7 hours   **Makes 1 serving**

- 15 g/½ oz/1 tbsp butter
- 1 small leek, trimmed and thinly sliced
- 50 g/2 oz button mushrooms, halved
- 175 g/6 oz sweet potato, peeled and cut into 2 cm/¾ in cubes
- 5 ml/1 tsp plain (all-purpose) flour
- 25 g/1 oz/2 tbsp cream cheese or Mascarpone cheese
- 100 ml/3½ fl oz/scant ½ cup vegetable stock

- salt and freshly ground black pepper

For the crumble topping

- 50 g/2 oz/½ cup plain flour
- 25 g/1 oz/2 tbsp butter
- 25 g/1 oz/¼ cup freshly grated Cheddar cheese
- 15 ml/1 tbsp chopped walnuts or mixed nuts
- 15 ml/1 tbsp rolled oats

1 Melt the butter in a frying pan, add the leek and mushrooms and cook gently for 5 minutes or until almost tender. Stir in the sweet potato.

2 Sprinkle the flour over the vegetables and stir in, then add the cream cheese or Mascarpone cheese. Gradually stir in the stock. Continue stirring over a low heat until the mixture is bubbling and thickened. Season to taste.

3 Leave to cool for 1 minute, then transfer the vegetable mixture to the ceramic cooking pot. Cover with the lid, switch on the slow cooker to Low and cook for 5–6 hours.

4 To make the crumble topping, sift the flour into a bowl and rub in the butter until the mixture resembles fine breadcrumbs. Stir in the cheese, nuts and oats. Spoon the topping over the vegetables, re-cover and cook for a further hour. If liked, brown the top under a moderate grill (broiler) until golden before serving.

Cook smart

- Sweet potatoes have a delicious rich flavour and work well in this dish but, if you prefer, a mixture of ordinary potatoes and carrots may be used instead.

Spiced Indian Rice

The cashew nuts in this mildly spiced rice dish add both protein and texture. You could double the ingredients and use the second portion to serve with a dish from the freezer the next day.

🕐 Cooking time: 1½ hours	👥 Makes 1 serving

- 10 ml/2 tsp groundnut (peanut) or sunflower oil
- 1 small onion, finely chopped
- 1 garlic clove, crushed
- 2.5 ml/½ tsp ground coriander (cilantro)
- 2.5 ml/½ tsp ground cumin
- a small pinch of ground turmeric

- 200 ml/8 fl oz/1 cup hot (not boiling) vegetable stock
- salt and freshly ground black pepper
- 75 g/3 oz/⅓ cup easy-cook (converted) rice
- 75 g/3 oz baby spinach leaves
- 25 g/1 oz/¼ cup unsalted cashew nuts, toasted

1 Heat the oil in a frying pan, add the onion and garlic and cook gently for 7–8 minutes until soft. Stir in the spices and cook for a further minute, stirring constantly. Turn off the heat and transfer the mixture to the ceramic cooking pot.

2 Pour the stock over the onion mixture and season with salt and pepper. Stir, then cover with the lid and switch on the slow cooker to High. Cook for 30 minutes, then stir in the rice, re-cover and cook for 35 minutes.

3 Lay the spinach on the surface of the rice, replace the lid and cook for a further 20–30 minutes or until the spinach has wilted and the rice is cooked and tender. Stir to mix the rice and spinach together. Serve at once, scattered with toasted cashew nuts.

Cook smart

- If baby spinach leaves are unavailable, use ordinary spinach leaves, removing any tough stalks and tearing the leaves into smaller pieces.

⌄ Couscous and Cheese Peppers

This bright, cheery dish has a real Mediterranean feel and flavour and can be served as a main course for one, or a light lunch or starter for two. Use sweet red or yellow peppers, as green ones may become bitter after long cooking.

🕐 **Cooking time: 2–4 hours**   👤 **Makes 1 serving**

- 1 red or yellow (bell) pepper
- 25 g/1 oz instant couscous
- 45 ml/3 tbsp boiling vegetable stock or water
- 10 ml/2 tsp olive oil
- 2 spring onions (scallions), trimmed and sliced
- 2 ripe tomatoes, peeled and chopped
- 15 ml/1 tbsp toasted pine kernels
- 3–4 stoned (pitted) black olives, roughly chopped
- 50 g/2 oz Feta cheese, crumbled or finely diced
- a small pinch of dried mixed herbs
- 5 ml/1 tsp lemon juice
- salt and freshly ground black pepper

1 Halve the pepper lengthways or widthways, depending on which will fit best in your slow cooker, then remove the core and seeds. Put the halves in a heatproof bowl and pour over enough boiling water to cover them. Leave for 3 minutes, then remove, reserving the water. Drain the peppers thoroughly and set aside.

2 Put the couscous in a small bowl and pour the stock over. Leave to stand for a few minutes. Heat the oil in a saucepan, add the spring onions and cook for 3–4 minutes until soft. Turn off the heat and stir in the remaining ingredients and the couscous, seasoning to taste with salt and pepper. Mix again.

3 Divide the mixture between the pepper halves, packing it tightly. Place filling-side up in the ceramic cooking pot, then pour in enough of the reserved pepper-soaking water to come to about a third of the way up the peppers.

4 Cover with the lid and switch on the slow cooker to High. Cook for 2–4 hours or until the peppers are really tender but still holding their shape. Carefully remove and serve at once.

˅ Creamy Risotto with Beans

This fragrant risotto makes a satisfying meal. The gentle heat of the slow cooker and a spoonful of Mascarpone cheese ensures a thick and creamy, but not heavy, texture to the finished dish. It goes down well with a glass of white wine!

Cooking time: 1½ hours   **Makes 1 serving**

- 10 ml/2 tsp olive oil
- 15 g/½ oz/1 tbsp butter, preferably unsalted (sweet)
- 1 small onion or 2 shallots, peeled and finely chopped
- 1 garlic clove, crushed
- 60 ml/4 tbsp dry white wine
- 375 ml/13 fl oz/1½ cups boiling vegetable stock

- 100 g/4 oz/½ cup easy-cook (converted) Italian risotto rice
- 2.5 ml/½ tsp fresh thyme or a pinch of dried thyme
- salt and freshly ground black pepper
- 1 x 200 g/7 oz/small can of cannellini beans, drained and rinsed
- 15 ml/1 tbsp Mascarpone cheese
- 25 g/1 oz/¼ cup freshly grated Parmesan cheese

1 Heat the oil and butter in a frying pan, add the onion or shallots and garlic and cook gently for 7–8 minutes or until really soft. Turn off the heat, then stir in the wine. Transfer the mixture to the ceramic cooking pot and switch on the slow cooker to High. Cover with the lid and cook for 30 minutes.

Cook smart

- Take care when seasoning this dish as Parmesan cheese is already quite salty.
- You could use extra stock instead of the wine.
- Borlotti beans may be substituted for the cannelloni beans in this recipe, if preferred.
- If you can't get a small can of cannellini beans, use half a 400 g/ 14 oz/large can. Main Meal Minestrone (see page 16) also contains cannellini beans.

2 Add the stock to the cooking pot, then stir in the rice and thyme and some salt and pepper. Re-cover and cook for a further 45 minutes, stirring once half-way through cooking. At this stage the rice should be almost tender and most of the liquid absorbed. If not, cook for further 10 minutes.

3 Stir in the beans and Mascarpone and cook for a final 15 minutes or until the rice is tender. Stir in half the Parmesan, then cover and leave to stand for 1–2 minutes. Stir again, then serve at once, sprinkled with the remaining Parmesan.

Vegetable Goulash

This easy, one-pot dish makes a nourishing main course and needs no accompaniments. It's perfect comfort food to enjoy on a cold, damp winter's day to warm you up after a long journey home from work in the dark.

Cooking time: 7–9 hours   **Makes 2 servings**

- 10 ml/2 tsp olive oil
- 1 small onion, peeled and chopped
- 1 garlic clove, crushed
- 10 ml/2 tsp paprika
- 175 g/6 oz small new potatoes, scrubbed
- 175 g/6 oz cauliflower florets
- 2 medium carrots, peeled and thickly sliced
- 1 acorn squash or ½ small butternut squash, seeds removed, peeled and diced
- ½ x 400 g/14 oz/large can of chick peas (garbanzos), drained
- 300 ml/½ pt/1¼ cups tomato juice
- 2.5 ml/½ tsp dried mixed herbs
- salt and freshly ground black pepper

To serve

- thick natural or Greek-style yoghurt

1 Heat the oil in a frying pan, add the onion and cook for 7–8 minutes or until soft. Stir in the garlic, then sprinkle the paprika over and cook for a few more seconds. Transfer the mixture to the ceramic cooking pot and switch on the slow cooker to Auto or High.

2 Add all the remaining ingredients and stir well. Cover with the lid and cook for 1 hour. Leave the slow cooker on Auto or reduce the temperature to Low and cook for a further 6–8 hours until the vegetables are tender.

3 Spoon half the goulash into a dish and leave to cool. Serve the remaining casserole at once, topped with a spoonful of yoghurt.

Second serving

Cover the cooled goulash and chill in the fridge for the following day. To serve, heat gently in a saucepan with a little extra tomato juice or stock until bubbling and hot.

Cook smart

- Use the rest of the canned chick peas to make Spanish Chorizo Soup (see page 18).

Desserts

*F*rom light fruit compôtes to creamy baked custards and decadent chocolate puddings, you'll find all manner of desserts here to suit every season and occasion. Try classic favourites such as Old-fashioned Rice Pudding or Baked Stuffed Apple, or indulge yourself with Panettone Pudding or Dark Chocolate Fondue.

As well as hot puddings, there are plenty of cold desserts that can be made well in advance. Some of these also make great breakfast or brunch dishes, including Ginger-spiced Rhubarb and Winter Dried Fruit Compôte. There's plenty of choice to satisfy anyone with a sweet tooth.

Panettone Pudding

This is a glamorous version of bread and butter pudding, with smooth egg custard and brandy-soaked dried fruit. Panettone is a traditional dome-shaped Italian sweet bread with citrus peel and sultanas that is almost a cake – delicious!

Cooking time: 3–5 hours

Makes 2 generous servings

- 25 g/1oz sultanas (golden raisins)
- 25 g/1 oz no-need-to-soak dried apricots, chopped
- 30 ml/2 tbsp brandy
- 25 g/1 oz/2 tbsp butter, preferably unsalted (sweet), softened
- 175 g/6 oz panettone, cut into medium slices

- 30 ml/2 tbsp apricot conserve
- 1 small egg, lightly beaten
- 200 ml/7 fl oz/scant 1 cup milk
- 5 ml/1 tsp vanilla essence (extract)
- 5 ml/1 tsp caster (superfine) sugar

To serve
- whipped cream

1 Put the sultanas and apricots in a small bowl, pour the brandy over and leave to soak for a few minutes. Place an upturned saucer or a metal pastry (paste) cutter in the base of the ceramic cooking pot and pour in about 2.5 cm/1 in hot (not boiling) water. Switch on the slow cooker to High.

2 Use a third of the butter to grease the base and sides of a 600 ml/1 pt/2½ cup heatproof dish, about 5 cm/2 in deep. Thinly spread the panettone slices with the remaining butter, then the conserve. Cut each slice diagonally into quarters. Arrange the slices in the dish, scattering the sultanas and apricots between the layers.

3 Whisk together the egg, milk, vanilla essence and any remaining soaking liquid. Slowly pour over the panettone, then gently press the slices down into the liquid. Cover with foil.

4 Place the dish on top of the saucer or pastry cutter, then pour in enough boiling water to come half-way up the dish. Cover with the lid and cook for 3–5 hours or until the custard is lightly set. Sprinkle the top with the sugar and serve half the pudding at once with whipped cream, if liked.

Second serving

Allow the rest of the pudding to cool in the dish. Cover and chill in the fridge for the following day. Serve cold – do not reheat.

Cook smart

- Use rum or milk instead of brandy.
- You'll find panettone in major supermarkets and delicatessens. Look for the tiny versions, which are ideal for this recipe.
- For an even richer pudding, make with half milk and half single (light) cream.
- You could make a more everyday version of this recipe by using up slightly stale ordinary white bread.

Caramel Coffee Custard

This lightly set, creamy-textured coffee custard is ideal for serving hot or cold. The topping is made simply by sprinkling Greek-style yoghurt with demerara sugar; it dissolves to a sticky caramel-like finish.

Cooking time: 3½ hours **Makes 1 serving**

- 150 ml/¼ pt/⅔ cup milk or half milk and half single (light) cream
- 1 egg
- 15 ml/1 tbsp soft light brown sugar

- 10 ml/2 tsp coffee essence (extract)
- 45 ml/3 tbsp Greek-style yoghurt
- 10 ml/2 tsp demerara sugar

1 Place an upturned saucer or a metal pastry (paste) cutter in the base of the ceramic cooking pot. Pour in about 2.5 cm/1 in hot (not boiling) water, then turn on the slow cooker to High.

2 Heat the milk or milk and cream mixture in a saucepan until it is steaming hot. Whisk together the egg, light brown sugar and coffee essence. Slowly pour over the hot milk, whisking all the time.

3 Pour the mixture into a 250 ml/ 8 fl oz /1 cup heatproof dish, cover with foil and place on top of the saucer or pastry cutter. Pour in enough boiling water to come half-way up the sides of the dish, cover with the lid and reduce the temperature to Low. Cook for 3 hours.

4 Remove the foil from the custard and spoon the yoghurt over the top, then sprinkle with the demerara sugar. Replace the foil and cook for a further 30 minutes to melt the sugar. Serve hot or chilled.

Cook smart
- If liked, make two desserts at the same time. For a variation, omit the coffee essence from one and flavour with 2.5 ml/½ tsp vanilla essence instead.

Old-fashioned Rice Pudding

This dessert is deliciously rich and creamy and, unlike oven-baked rice puddings, it doesn't form a thick skin on the top. Because little liquid escapes from the slow cooker during cooking, it's made with evaporated milk.

Cooking time: 3–8 hours   **Makes 2 servings**

- 15 g/½ oz/1 tbsp butter, softened
- 40 g/1½ oz pudding rice, rinsed and drained
- 25 g/1 oz/2 tbsp caster (superfine) sugar, or to taste
- 375 ml/13 fl oz/1½ cups evaporated milk
- a pinch of freshly grated nutmeg (optional)

To serve
- soft brown sugar, honey or jam (conserve)

1 Use the butter to grease the base and about a third of the way up the sides of the ceramic cooking pot. Add the rice, sugar and evaporated milk. Stir, then cover with the lid.

2 Cook on High for 3–4 hours, or on Low for 6–8 hours, stirring once or twice during the final 2 hours and adding the nutmeg, if using. The pudding is ready when the rice is tender and has absorbed most of the milk.

Cook smart

● For a chocolate rice pudding, sprinkle the cooked hot pudding with 25 g/1 oz/¼ cup plain (semi-sweet) or milk (sweet) chocolate drops and stir just before serving.

● For a less rich pudding, make with part evaporated and part full-fat milk.

3 Spoon half the pudding into a bowl and serve at once, sprinkled with a little soft brown sugar or drizzled with honey or with a spoonful of jam, if liked. Leave the remaining pudding to cool in the ceramic cooking pot, then transfer to a bowl.

Second serving

Cover the cold pudding and chill in the fridge for the following day. Serve cold, or reheat gently in a saucepan until piping hot.

Ginger-spiced Rhubarb

Rhubarb cooks to perfection in the slow cooker and makes a great breakfast compôte as well as a dessert. Ginger and orange are traditional flavourings because they perfectly complement its delicate flavour.

Cooking time: 1½–2 hours

Makes 2 servings

- 100 ml/3½ fl oz/scant ½ cup hot (not boiling) water
- a thinly pared strip of orange peel
- 5 ml/1 tsp finely chopped fresh root ginger
- 1 star anise or a small piece of cinnamon stick (optional)

- 100 g/4 oz/½ cup caster (superfine) sugar
- 225 g/8 oz rhubarb

To serve

- custard

1 Pour the water into the ceramic cooking pot. Add the orange peel, ginger, star anise or cinnamon stick, if using, and sugar. Switch on the slow cooker to High, cover with the lid and cook for 1 hour, stirring once or twice to dissolve the sugar.

2 Meanwhile, trim the rhubarb and cut into 2.5 cm/1 in pieces. Add to the hot syrup, cover and reduce the temperature to Low. Cook for ½–1 hour or until the rhubarb is tender but still holding its shape. Remove the orange peel and star anise or cinnamon. Spoon half the rhubarb into a dish and allow to cool. Serve the remainder at once with hot custard.

Second serving

Cover the cooled rhubarb and chill in the fridge for the following day. Serve with Greek yoghurt. Alternatively, fold the rhubarb and 15 ml/1 tbsp of the syrup into 150 ml/¼ pt/⅔ cup chilled fresh custard to make a rhubarb fool.

Cook smart

- Rhubarb is at its best in late winter and early spring when it has a light pink colour and a delicate flavour. Later, main-crop rhubarb has a deep red colour and is more tart, so may require extra sugar.

Tropical Fruit Crumble

This is a great way to jazz up the simple banana. If you like, you can make a double quantity of the crumble topping and freeze half for another day, ready to sprinkle on almost any combinations of fruit you like.

Cooking time: 1 hour **Makes 1 serving**

- 30 ml/2 tbsp soft brown sugar
- 15 ml/1 tbsp dark rum
- 1 banana
- 25 g/1 oz/¼ cup plain (all-purpose) flour
- 25 g/1 oz/¼ cup porridge oats
- 15 ml/1 tbsp desiccated (shredded) coconut
- 25 g/1 oz/2 tbsp butter, melted

To serve

- whipped cream or ice cream

1 Put half the sugar and the rum in the ceramic cooking pot. Switch on the slow cooker to High and cook for 15 minutes, stirring once or twice.

2 Peel and thickly slice the banana. Add to the sugar mixture and gently stir until all the slices are coated. Cover with the lid and cook for 45 minutes or until very soft. Spoon the bananas into a gratin or shallow heatproof dish.

3 While the bananas are cooking, mix together the flour, oats, the remaining sugar and the coconut. Stir in the melted butter to make a crumbly mixture. Sprinkle over the bananas and cook under a moderate grill (broiler) for 3–4 minutes until golden brown. Serve at once with whipped cream or ice cream.

Spiced Mulled Pears

This is a great way to use up red wine left over from the night before but, if you prefer, apple juice or plain water may be used to make the syrup. You can of course, leave out the spices if you don't have any to hand.

Cooking time: 3–4 hours | **Makes 2 servings**

- 50 g/2 oz/¼ cup caster (superfine) sugar
- 175 ml/6 fl oz/¾ cup red wine
- a thinly pared strip of orange peel
- ½ cinnamon stick
- 2 whole cloves
- 3 small pears or 2 medium ones

To serve

- whipped cream

1 Put the sugar, wine, orange peel and spices in the ceramic cooking pot. Cover with the lid and switch on the slow cooker to High. Cook for 1 hour.

2 Meanwhile, quarter, core and peel the pears. Add to the wine mixture, re-cover and cook on High for 1 hour, or reduce the temperature to Low and cook for 2–3 hours until tender. Remove the orange peel and spices.

3 Spoon half the pears and syrup into a bowl and leave to cool. Serve the rest at once with whipped cream, if liked.

Second serving

Cover the cooled pears and chill in the fridge for the following day. Serve chilled, or reheat gently in a saucepan until piping hot.

> **Cook smart**
> ● If you prefer a thicker syrup, spoon the pears into a bowl as at step 3 and keep warm. Strain the syrup into a pan and simmer briskly on the hob until reduced by about half.

Baked Stuffed Apple

I recommend that you use an eating apple for this dish because the fruit is crisper and will hold its shape. If you do use a cooking apple, select a variety that won't break down and collapse during the long, slow cooking.

Cooking time: 3 hours

Makes 1 serving

- 20 g/¾ oz/1½ tbsp butter, preferably unsalted (sweet), softened
- 30 ml/2 tbsp apple or orange juice
- 15 g/½ oz/1 tbsp soft light brown sugar
- 5 ml/1 tsp finely grated lemon or orange zest
- 1.5 ml/¼ tsp ground cinnamon

- 25 g/1 oz dried cranberries, glacé (candied) cherries or mixed glacé fruit, chopped
- 1 large eating (dessert) or small cooking (tart) apple

To serve

- cream, crème fraîche or vanilla ice cream

1 Use a third of the butter to grease the base of the ceramic cooking pot. Pour in the fruit juice and switch on the slow cooker to High. Put the rest of the butter in a mixing bowl with the sugar, citrus zest and cinnamon. Beat together, then stir in the chopped fruit.

2 Cut a thin slice from the base of the apple so that it will stand upright. Remove the core using an apple corer, then carefully enlarge the cavity slightly so that it will hold the filling.

3 Spoon the filling into the cavity, then place the apple in the slow cooker and cover with the lid. Reduce the temperature to Low and cook for 3 hours or until tender. Serve on a warmed plate or bowl with cream, crème fraîche or ice cream.

Butterscotch Apples

Although this dessert contains only four ingredients, it will satisfy your sweet cravings and is well worth the wait. For a really decadent dish, serve with a good-quality vanilla ice cream, which will melt into the butterscotch sauce.

Cooking time: 1¼–1½ hours | **Makes 1 serving**

- 20 g/¾ oz/1½ tbsp butter
- 30 ml/2 tbsp golden (light corn) syrup
- 25 g/1 oz/2 tbsp demerara sugar
- 1 eating (dessert) apple, quartered, cored and peeled

To serve

- ice cream, whipped cream or Greek-style yoghurt

1 Put the butter, syrup and sugar in the ceramic cooking pot, cover with a lid and switch on the slow cooker to High. Cook for 30 minutes, stirring once half-way through to combine the ingredients.

2 Stir until the sugar has dissolved, then add the apple quarters and stir again to coat in the mixture. Cover and cook for a further ¾–1 hour or until the apples are translucent and tender and the sauce is sticky.

3 Turn off the slow cooker and allow to cool for a few minutes before serving with ice cream, whipped cream or a large spoonful of Greek-style yoghurt.

Winter Dried Fruit Compôte

You can buy mixed dried apples, pears and peaches in a single packet, or alternatively just use your favourites. They are cooked slowly in an apple and orange syrup, sweetened with honey and scented with cinnamon to make a healthy dessert.

Cooking time: 6–8 hours   **Makes 2 servings**

- 1 large orange
- 300 ml/½ pt/1¼ cups apple juice
- 15 ml/1 tbsp clear honey
- ½ cinnamon stick

- 250 g/9 oz dried fruit such as apples, pears, peaches, apricots, prunes, figs, blueberries, cherries or cranberries

To serve

- custard

1 Pare a long strip of zest from the orange and put in the ceramic cooking pot with the remaining ingredients. Cover with the lid and switch on the slow cooker to Low.

2 Cook for 6–8 hours or until the fruit is very tender and much of the liquid has absorbed. Turn off the heat.

3 Halve the orange, squeeze out the juice and stir into the compôte. Spoon half into a bowl and serve hot with custard.

Second serving

Transfer the remaining compôte to a bowl and leave to cool. Cover and chill in the fridge for the following day. Serve cold or at room temperature with Greek-style yoghurt.

Cook smart

- For a tropical fruit compôte, include chunks of dried mango and pineapple.

ᵛHoneyed Rosemary Apricots

Dried apricots are a great source of vitamins and minerals as the drying process boosts their levels of vitamin C, beta carotene and iron. In this dessert, they're flavoured with rosemary, which gives them a wonderful, aromatic fragrance.

🕐 Cooking time: 3 hours	👥 Makes 2 servings

- 1 lime
- 15 ml/1 tbsp clear honey
- a sprig of fresh rosemary
- 175 g/6 oz/1 cup no-need-to-soak dried apricots

- 150 ml/¼ pt/⅔ cup hot (not boiling) water

To serve
- Greek-style yoghurt

1 Pare a thin strip of peel from the lime and put in the ceramic cooking pot. Add the remaining ingredients and switch on the slow cooker to Low.

2 Cover with the lid and cook for 3 hours or until the apricots are really tender. Turn off the slow cooker and leave to cool. Squeeze the juice from the lime and stir into the syrup.

3 Serve half the apricots and syrup warm or cold with Greek-style yoghurt. Put the remainder in a bowl, cover and chill in the fridge.

◎ Second serving

Serve the rest of the honeyed apricots cold. They will keep in the fridge for up to 3 days.

ɤ Dark Chocolate Fondue

This is a truly decadent dessert for when you really want to spoil yourself. It also makes a great treat for sharing, if you double up the quantities. You can really let your imagination run away with you in your choice of dippers.

🕐 **Cooking time: 30 minutes**   👥 **Makes 1 serving**

- 75 ml/3 fl oz/5 tbsp double (heavy) cream
- 10 ml/2 tsp orange or coffee liqueur or brandy (optional)
- 75 g/3 oz dark (semi-sweet) chocolate, chopped

To serve

- fresh fruit for dipping such as small whole strawberries, large seedless grapes, satsuma segments, kiwi slices; marshmallows; cubed plain cake

1 Pour the cream into the ceramic cooking pot and switch on the slow cooker to High. Stir in the liqueur or brandy, cover with the lid and heat for 30 minutes.

2 Sprinkle the chocolate over the hot cream. Stir until melted and blended, then reduce the temperature to Low.

3 Serve at once, or keep warm for up to 30 minutes. For a thicker fondue, turn off the heat and allow to cool for 10 minutes before serving.

❮ Baked Chocolate Mousse

A wickedly rich dessert to satisfy even the most self-indulgent chocoholic, though it uses mainly storecupboard ingredients. The mousses should still be a little wobbly when cooked as the mixture will thicken and set as it cools.

🕐 Cooking time: 3 hours

👥 Makes 2 servings

- butter for greasing
- 1 egg
- 15 ml/1 tbsp caster (superfine) sugar
- 15 ml/1 tbsp cocoa (unsweetened chocolate) powder

- 150 ml/¼ pt/⅔ cup milk
- 75 ml/3 fl oz/5 tbsp double (heavy) cream
- 2.5 ml/½ tsp vanilla essence (extract)

1 Lightly grease two 150 ml/¼ pt/ ⅔ cup ramekins (custard cups). Pour about 2.5 cm/1 in hot (not boiling) water into the base of the ceramic cooking pot and switch on the slow cooker to Low.

2 Beat the egg with the sugar and cocoa powder until blended. Slightly warm the milk, cream and vanilla essence in a pan, then pour over the egg mixture, beating well. Divide between the ramekins, cover with clingfilm (plastic wrap) and place in the cooking pot.

3 Pour in enough near-boiling water to come just over half-way up the sides of the dishes. Cover with the lid and cook for 3 hours or until lightly set. Remove from the cooking pot and leave to cool, then chill in the fridge for at least 1 hour.

◎ Second serving

If liked, turn the second serving into a chocolate crème brulee – but make sure the dish is heatproof before you do this! Sprinkle the top evenly with 30 ml/2 tbsp golden caster sugar, then place under a preheated moderate grill (broiler) and cook until the sugar melts and caramelises. Cool before serving.

⌄ Chocolate Almond Pudding

You can add even more chocolate and nuts to this wicked pudding if you are feeling really indulgent by stirring in a handful of white chocolate chips and a few chopped almonds before cooking at step 4.

Cooking time: 2–4 hours **Makes 2 generous servings**

- 50 g/2 oz/¼ cup butter, softened, plus extra for greasing
- 50 g/2 oz/½ cup chopped plain (semisweet) chocolate
- 50 g/2 oz/¼ cup light soft brown sugar
- 1 egg, lightly beaten
- 50 g/2 oz/½ cup self-raising flour

- 15 ml/1 tbsp cocoa (unsweetened chocolate) powder
- 15 g/½ oz ground almonds
- 15 ml/1 tbsp milk
- 10 ml/2 tsp icing (confectioners') sugar

To serve

- custard or ice cream

1 Lightly grease a 450 ml/¾ pt/2 cup heatproof baking dish. Pour about 5 cm/2 in hot (not boiling) water into the base of the ceramic cooking pot. Switch on the slow cooker to High.

2 Put the chocolate in a heatproof bowl. Place in the slow cooker and leave for about 10 minutes, stirring occasionally, until the chocolate has melted. Remove and leave to cool for about 5 minutes. Place an upturned saucer or a metal pastry (paste) cutter in the base of the ceramic cooking pot.

3 Put the butter and sugar in a bowl and beat together until light and fluffy. Add the egg, a little at a time and beating after each addition. Sift the flour and cocoa over the creamed mixture, add the ground almonds and melted chocolate and gently fold together. When half-mixed, add the milk and mix to a soft consistency.

4 Spoon the mixture into the prepared dish and level the top. Cover loosely with a piece of buttered foil. Place in the cooking pot on top of the saucer or pastry cutter and, if necessary, pour in a little more hot water to come half-way up the sides of the dish.

5 Cover with the lid and cook for 2–4 hours or until the pudding is well-risen and firm. Dust with the icing sugar before serving half the pudding with custard or ice cream. Allow the remaining pudding to cool.

ⓒ Second serving

Serve the second portion of pudding cold with some red berry fruit such as raspberries and a generous helping of Greek-style yoghurt or whipped cream.

Marmalade Ginger Pudding

You can use thin- or thick-cut marmalade for this pudding, depending on your preference. Or try different flavours such as lime, or the orange and whisky marmalade you'll find in the preserves in the following chapter.

Cooking time: 2–4 hours **Makes 2 servings**

- 50 g/2 oz/¼ cup butter, softened, plus extra for greasing
- 30 ml/2 tbsp marmalade
- 50 g/2 oz/¼ cup caster (superfine) sugar
- 1 egg, lightly beaten

- 50 g/2 oz/½ cup self-raising flour
- 15 g/½ oz stem ginger, finely chopped
- 15 ml/1 tbsp orange juice or milk

To serve

- custard or cream

1 Grease a 600 ml/1 pt/2½ cup pudding basin, then line the base with a circle of non-stick baking parchment. Spoon in the marmalade. Place an upturned saucer or metal pastry (paste) cutter in the base of the ceramic cooking pot and pour in about 2.5 cm/1 in hot (not boiling) water. Switch on the slow cooker to High.

2 Put the butter and sugar in a bowl and beat together until creamy. Add the egg, a little at a time and beating after each addition. Sift the flour over the mixture, then gently fold in with the ginger and orange juice or milk.

3 Spoon the mixture into the prepared basin. Cover the pudding with a piece of pleated, lightly greased baking parchment, followed by pleated foil, tucking the excess paper and foil tightly under the rim. Place the pudding on the saucer or pastry cutter. Pour in enough boiling water to come half-way up the sides of the basin.

4 Cover with the lid and cook for 2–4 hours or until the pudding is well risen and firm. Turn out the pudding and remove the lining paper. Serve half hot with custard or cream.

Second serving

Allow the second portion of pudding to cool, then cover and keep in the fridge for the following day. Reheat in an ovenproof dish covered with foil in a low oven, or covered with clingfilm (plastic wrap) in a microwave.

Chocolate and Orange Pudding

Follow the recipe but replace the ginger with 5 ml/1 tsp finely grated orange zest, and 15 g/½ oz of the flour with 15 g/½ oz cocoa (unsweetened chocolate) powder.

Jam-capped Sponge

Follow the recipe but omit the ginger and replace the marmalade with raspberry or blackcurrant jam (conserve).

Coffee Pudding

Follow the recipe but omit the ginger and replace the orange juice or milk with 10 ml/2 tsp coffee essence (extract) blended with 5 ml/1 tsp milk.

⌄ Light Christmas Pudding

Although you can easily buy individual traditional-style Christmas puddings, they tend to be not very exciting. This is a really special fruity version with a lighter colour and texture and will be far better than anything shop-bought.

🕐 **Cooking time: 7–9 hours** 👥 **Makes 2 generous servings**

- 100 g/4 oz/⅔ cup luxury dried mixed fruit (fruit cake mix)
- 50 g/2 oz/⅓ cup stoned (pitted) ready-to-eat dried dates, chopped
- 25 g/1 oz dried cranberries
- finely grated zest and juice of ½ small orange
- 30 ml/2 tbsp orange liqueur or brandy (or extra orange juice)
- 5 ml/1 tsp grated fresh root ginger or 2.5 ml/½ tsp ground ginger
- 40 g/1½ oz/3 tbsp butter, softened, plus extra for greasing

- 40 g/1½ oz/3 tbsp dark soft brown sugar
- 1 small egg, lightly beaten
- 15 g/½ oz/2 tbsp self-raising flour
- 25 g/1 oz/½ cup fresh white breadcrumbs
- 25 g/1 oz/¼ cup chopped walnuts or pecan nuts
- 2.5 ml/½ tsp ground cinnamon

To serve
- brandy butter, custard or cream

1 Put the dried fruits, orange zest and juice, liqueur or brandy and ginger in the ceramic cooking pot. Stir, then switch on the slow cooker to Low, cover with the lid and cook for 1 hour. Turn off, then transfer the mixture to a bowl, cover and leave to cool. Wash up the ceramic cooking pot.

2 Lightly grease a 450 ml/¾ pt/2 cup pudding basin and line the base with a circle of non-stick baking parchment. Place an upturned saucer or metal pastry (paste) cutter in the base of the clean ceramic cooking pot and pour in about 2.5 cm/1 in hot (not boiling) water. Switch on the slow cooker to High.

3 Put the butter and sugar in a bowl and beat together until creamy. Add the egg and flour a little at a time, beating after each addition. Stir in the breadcrumbs, nuts, cinnamon and cooled fruits.

4 Spoon the mixture into the prepared pudding basin and level the top. Cover with a piece of pleated lightly greased greaseproof (waxed) paper, followed by pleated foil. Tie round the rim securely with string and place in the cooking pot on top of the saucer or pastry cutter. Pour in enough boiling water to come half-way up the basin.

5 Cover with the lid and cook for 6–8 hours. Remove from the slow cooker and leave to cool, then store in a cool place for up to 1 week, or freeze for 1 month. To serve, allow the pudding to come to room temperature, then cook as above in the slow cooker on Auto or High for 1 hour, then keep warm on Low for up to 4 hours. Serve hot with brandy butter, custard or cream.

Cook smart

● If you prefer, step 1 can be done on the hob. Put the ingredients in a small pan, then warm gently for about 10 minutes, stirring occasionally, until the liquid is absorbed.

● Any type of 'luxury' dried fruit can be used for this pudding. Look out for those with glacé (candied) cherries and chopped dried apricots in the mixture or, for a slightly more exotic flavour, with passion fruit and pineapple.

● To make brandy butter, cream 50 g/2 oz/¼ cup softened unsalted (sweet) butter with 65 g/2½ oz/⅓ cup light soft brown or muscovado sugar. Beat in 30 ml/2 tbsp brandy.

● So that you can easily lift the pudding out of the slow cooker, put a long strip of folded foil under the basin and around the sides to use as a handle.

Cakes, preserves and drinks

*L*emon Drizzle Cake with a sugary topping and a dark Rich Chocolate Cake with a creamy chocolate frosting; these are treats to rival any shop-bought confection.

Many cakes can be made successfully in a slow cooker. Moist mixtures such as carrot cake and gingerbread work especially well as they require long cooking at a low temperature. These types of cake are usually allowed to mature before eating, but this isn't necessary when they are made in the slow cooker. Light-textured sponges can also be made, but not whisked sponges as these need fast cooking at a high temperature. Cakes cooked in the slow cooker darken in colour, but they do not brown in the same way as an oven-baked cake, so there are plenty of suggestions for icing or decorating them as well. However, if you prefer, you can finish them by sprinkling with a few chopped or flaked nuts before cooking, or by simply dusting with icing (confectioners') sugar afterwards.

Although the slow cooker isn't suitable for fast-boiling jams and marmalades to setting point, it is perfect for making rich chutneys, as the long cooking time develops the flavour, making long maturation unnecessary. It's also incredibly easy to make fruit curds, such as Tangy Lemon Curd, as there's no need for constant stirring.

The slow cooker is excellent for infusing spices and keeping hot punches and drinks warm. Try serving a glass of steaming mulled wine or a refreshing chilled fruit punch next time you're entertaining.

Lemon Drizzle Cake

This light lemony sponge is drizzled with a thick, sticky syrup while it is still warm, so that a sugary crust forms on top of the cake. It's lovely with coffee in the morning or a cup of tea mid-afternoon, but it also makes a delicious dessert.

🕐 **Cooking time: 2–3 hours**   👥 **Makes 3–4 servings**

For the cake
- 50 g/2 oz/¼ cup soft margarine, plus extra for greasing
- 50 g/2 oz/¼ cup caster (superfine) sugar
- 1 egg
- 50 g/2 oz/½ cup self-raising flour
- 1.5 ml/¼ tsp baking power

- finely grated zest of ½ lemon
- 10 ml/2 tsp milk

For the lemon syrup topping
- a thinly pared strip of lemon peel
- juice of ½ lemon
- 45 ml/3 tbsp caster (superfine) sugar

1 Place an upturned saucer or metal pastry (paste) cutter in the base of the ceramic cooking pot and pour in about 2.5 cm/1 in hot (not boiling) water. Switch on the slow cooker to High. Grease a 13–15 cm/5–6 in round fixed-base cake tin or soufflé dish and line the base with greaseproof (waxed) paper or baking parchment.

2 Put all the cake ingredients in a bowl and beat with a wooden spoon until smooth and creamy.

◎ **Cook smart**

- You can also make this cake with light muscovado or soft brown sugar and self-raising wholemeal flour.
- The cake will keep for 2–3 days in an airtight tin or container. Alternatively, wrap in greaseproof paper, then in foil and freeze for up to a month.

3 Spoon the mixture into the prepared tin or dish and level the top. Cover with lightly greased foil and place in the cooking pot on top of the saucer or pastry cutter. Pour in enough boiling water to come half-way up the tin or dish.

4 Cover with the lid and cook for 2–3 hours or until the cake is firm and a skewer inserted into the middle comes out clean. Carefully remove and allow to stand on a wire rack for 5 minutes before turning out. Peel off the lining paper and leave the cake to cool for 5 minutes.

5 Meanwhile, to make the topping, put the lemon peel, lemon juice and sugar in a small pan and heat gently until the sugar has dissolved. Bring to the boil and simmer for about 30 seconds. Cool for a few minutes, then remove the peel and drizzle the hot syrup over the cooling cake. Leave until completely cold before slicing.

Rich Chocolate Cake

This dark chocolate cake, slowly steamed in the slow cooker, surpasses any oven-baked version and is beautifully moist and even-textured. A creamy chocolate frosting, which is well worth the effort, adds the final flourish.

Cooking time: 2 hours	Makes 3–4 servings

For the cake

- 65 g/2½ oz/⅓ cup butter, softened, plus extra for greasing
- 40 g/1½ oz soft light brown sugar
- 15 g/½ oz clear honey
- 1 egg, lightly beaten
- 50 g/2 oz/½ cup self-raising flour
- 15 g/½ oz /1½ tbsp cocoa (unsweetened chocolate) powder
- 1.5 ml/¼ tsp baking powder
- 5 ml/1 tsp milk
- 2.5 ml/½ tsp vanilla essence (extract)

For the frosting

- 100 g/4 oz plain (semi-sweet) chocolate
- 100 ml/3½ fl oz/scant ½ cup double (heavy) cream

1 Place an upturned saucer or metal pastry (paste) cutter in the base of the ceramic cooking pot and pour in about 2.5 cm/1 in hot (not boiling) water. Switch on the slow cooker to High. Grease a 13–15 cm/5–6 in round fixed-base cake tin or soufflé dish and line the base with greaseproof (waxed) paper or baking parchment.

2 To make the cake, put the butter, sugar and honey in a mixing bowl and beat together until light and fluffy. Gradually beat in the egg, a little at a time. Sift the flour, cocoa powder and baking powder into the bowl and fold in with the milk and vanilla essence.

3 Spoon and scrape the mixture into the prepared tin or dish and level the top. Cover with lightly greased foil and place in the cooking pot on top of the saucer or pastry cutter. Pour in enough boiling water to come half-way up the sides of the dish or tin.

4 Cover with the lid and cook for 2 hours or until the cake is well risen and firm and a skewer inserted into the middle comes out clean. Carefully remove from the slow cooker and stand on a cooling rack for 5 minutes before turning out and leaving to cool.

5 Meanwhile, to make the chocolate frosting, turn off the slow cooker but leave the hot water in the cooking pot. Break the chocolate into squares and place in a heatproof bowl with the cream. Lower the bowl into the hot water in the cooking pot (the water should come between a third and half-way up the bowl) and leave for a few minutes, then stir until the chocolate has melted and combined with the cream.

6 Remove the bowl and let the frosting cool. Put in the fridge for $^3/_4$–1 hour, stirring it every now and then as it thickens. When it is a thick consistency, spread over the top and sides of the cooled cake. Chill in the fridge until set.

Cook smart
- The cake will keep for up to 3 days in an airtight tin or other container.

℣ Carrot and Coconut Cake

If you can't resist the lure of a slice of cake smothered in creamy icing, but want a relatively healthy treat, this moist carrot cake provides the perfect solution. It's one of my favourites and I think it will be yours too!

Cooking time: 3–5 hours	Makes 2 servings

For the cake

- 25 g/1 oz sultanas (golden raisins)
- 10 ml/2 tsp orange or apple juice or milk
- 50 g/2 oz/¼ cup butter or margarine, at room temperature, plus extra for greasing
- 50 g/2 oz/¼ cup soft light brown sugar
- 1 egg, lightly beaten
- 50 g/2 oz carrots, trimmed, peeled and grated
- 15 g/½ oz desiccated (shredded) coconut

- 50 g/2 oz/½ cup self-raising flour
- 1.5 ml/¼ tsp baking powder
- 1.5 ml/¼ tsp ground cinnamon
- a small pinch of salt (optional)

For the icing (frosting)

- 75 g/3 oz/⅓ cup Mascarpone or low-fat cream cheese
- 2.5 ml/½ tsp finely grated orange zest (optional)
- 10 ml/2 tsp icing (confectioners') sugar, sifted

1 Put the sultanas in a small bowl, spoon the fruit juice or milk over and set aside to soak. Place an upturned saucer or metal pastry (paste) cutter in the base of the ceramic cooking pot and pour in about 2.5cm/1 in hot (not boiling) water. Turn on the slow cooker to High. Grease a 13–15 cm/ 5–6 in round fixed-base cake tin or soufflé dish and line the base with greaseproof (waxed) paper or baking parchment.

2 To make the cake, put the butter or margarine and sugar in a mixing bowl and beat until light and fluffy. Beat in the egg, a little at a time. Stir in the carrots, coconut and sultanas with their soaking liquid.

3 Sift the flour, baking powder, cinnamon and salt, if using, over the mixture and gently fold in. Spoon and scrape the mixture into the prepared tin or dish and level the top. Cover with lightly greased foil and place in the cooking pot on top of the saucer or pastry cutter.

4 Pour in enough boiling water to come about half-way up the sides of the tin or dish. Cover with the lid and cook for 3–5 hours or until a skewer inserted into the middle comes out clean. Carefully remove from the slow cooker and allow to stand on a cooling rack for 10 minutes, then turn out and leave to cool. Peel off the lining paper.

5 To make the icing, beat together the cheese, orange zest, if using, and icing sugar in a bowl until smooth. Spread over the top of the cake, swirling it attractively. Chill in the fridge until ready to serve.

Cook smart

● The iced cake will keep in the fridge in an airtight container for 2–3 days. Left un-iced, it will keep for up to 5 days.

● If preferred, chopped pecans or walnuts may be used instead of the coconut.

● The un-iced cake is also good served hot with creamy custard as a dessert.

Sticky Gingerbread

Made conventionally, gingerbread should be kept for a day or two before eating to improve the flavour. This isn't necessary when it's cooked in the slow cooker, as the long cooking ensures that it matures and can be eaten straight away.

Cooking time: 4–5 hours

Makes 3–4 servings

- 50 g/2 oz/¼ cup butter, plus extra for greasing
- 75 g/3 oz/⅓ cup soft light brown sugar
- 50 g/2 oz golden (light corn) syrup
- 25 g/1 oz black treacle or molasses
- 75 g/3 oz/¾ cup self-raising flour
- 5 ml/1 tsp ground ginger
- a pinch of salt (optional)
- 1 egg, lightly beaten
- 1.5 ml/¼ tsp bicarbonate of soda (baking soda)
- 100 ml/3½ fl oz/scant ½ cup milk

1 Pour about 5 cm/2 in hot (not boiling) water into the ceramic cooking pot, then switch on the slow cooker to High. Grease a 13–15 cm/5–6 in round fixed-base cake tin or soufflé dish and line the base with greaseproof (waxed) paper or baking parchment.

2 Put the butter, sugar, syrup and treacle or molasses in a heatproof bowl that will fit in the ceramic cooking pot. Put in the cooking pot and leave for about 20 minutes or until melted. Remove and stir the melted ingredients together. Place an upturned saucer or metal pastry (paste) cutter in the base of the slow cooker.

3 Sift the flour, ginger and salt, if using, over the melted mixture and stir together, then stir in the beaten egg. Stir the bicarbonate of soda into the milk, then stir into the flour mixture. Pour into the prepared tin or dish and cover with lightly greased foil. Place in the cooking pot on top of the saucer or pastry cutter.

4 Pour in enough boiling water to come about half-way up the sides of the tin or dish. Cover with the lid and cook for 4–5 hours or until a skewer inserted into the middle comes out clean. Carefully remove from the slow cooker and allow to stand on a cooling rack for 10 minutes, then turn out and leave to cool. Peel off the lining paper.

Cook smart

- This gingerbread will keep in an airtight container for up to 5 days. The texture will improve and become stickier with keeping.
- Gingerbread looks really attractive if dusted with a little icing (confectioners') sugar before serving.

Mulled Wine

There's nothing more welcoming than a steaming glass of mulled wine, and the beauty of the slow cooker is that it can be made a couple of hours or so in advance of your guests' expected arrival and kept at the ideal temperature.

Cooking time: 2 hours

Makes 4 servings

- 25 g/1 oz/2 tbsp caster (superfine) sugar
- 75 ml/3 fl oz/5 tbsp very hot (not boiling) water
- 2 whole cloves

- 1 small orange
- ½ cinnamon stick
- ¾ x 70cl bottle of fruity red wine
- 45 ml/3 tbsp brandy or orange liqueur

1 Put the sugar in the ceramic cooking pot and pour the hot water over. Stir until the sugar has dissolved, then switch on the slow cooker to Low.

2 Press the cloves into the orange and add with the cinnamon and wine. Cover with the lid and heat for 2 hours.

3 Stir in the brandy or orange liqueur. The mulled wine is now ready to serve and can be kept hot for a further 2 hours. To serve, ladle into heatproof glasses.

Cook smart

- If you don't have heatproof glasses, warm ordinary wine glasses by rinsing them with warm water before adding the punch. Another way to prevent glasses from cracking is to place a teaspoon in them while you ladle in the hot drink.

- To make gluhwein, the popular hot German punch, leave out the water, brandy and liqueur and replace the caster sugar with soft, light brown sugar. Instead of an orange, stud the cloves into half a lemon. Cut the remaining lemon half into slices and float on top.

Chilled Fruit Punch

When entertaining, it's sensible to have non-alcoholic drinks available. This is a deliciously refreshing punch for those who'd like something a little more exciting than orange juice. Make the lime and ginger syrup in advance and keep chilled.

Cooking time: 2 hours, plus chilling Makes 3–4 servings

- 1 lime
- 2.5 cm/1 in piece of fresh root ginger, peeled and sliced
- 25 g/1 oz/2 tbsp caster (superfine) sugar
- 120 ml/4 fl oz/½ cup hot (not boiling) water

- 350 ml/12 fl oz/1⅓ cups clear apple juice

To serve

- crushed ice and chilled sparkling mineral water or soda water

1 Pare off two thin strips of lime peel and place in the ceramic cooking pot with the ginger, sugar and hot water. Cover with the lid and switch on the slow cooker to Auto or High. After 1 hour, reduce the temperature to Low or leave on Auto. Heat for a further 1 hour, then switch off the slow cooker and leave to cool.

2 Half the lime, then cut a few slices from one of the halves and set aside. Squeeze out the juice from the other lime half and add to the lime and ginger syrup. Strain the syrup into a jug, stir in the apple juice, cover and chill in the fridge for at least an hour.

3 To serve, pour the punch over plenty of crushed ice in glasses. Top up with a little sparkling mineral or soda water. Decorate each glass with a slice of lime.

Tangy Lemon Curd

This much-loved preserve is wonderful spread on buttered fresh bread, toast or crumpets. It's also good warmed and served as a sauce with steamed puddings. It really is worth making your own for the fresh lemon flavour.

🕐 **Cooking time: 1¼–2¼ hours**   👥 **Makes one 175 g/6 oz jar**

- finely grated zest and juice of 1 large lemon
- 75 g/3 oz/⅓ cup caster (superfine) sugar

- 40 g/1½ oz/3 tbsp unsalted (sweet) butter, diced
- 1 egg
- 1 egg yolk

1 Pour about 5 cm/2 in hot (not boiling) water into the ceramic cooking pot and switch on the slow cooker to High. Put the lemon zest and juice, sugar and butter in a heatproof bowl and place in the slow cooker.

2 Pour in enough near-boiling water to come about half-way up the side of the bowl. Leave for about 15 minutes, stirring occasionally, until the sugar has dissolved and the butter has melted. Reduce the temperature to Low.

3 Whisk together the egg and yolk in a jug with a fork. Strain through a sieve into the lemon mixture, then whisk to combine. Cover the bowl with clingfilm (plastic wrap), then cover the slow cooker with the lid.

4 Cook for 1–2 hours, whisking the mixture with a fork every 15 minutes. The lemon curd is ready when it is thick enough to coat the back of a wooden spoon.

5 Remove from the cooking pot and pour or spoon into a hot sterilised jar. Allow to cool, then cover and seal.

6 Store in the fridge. Unopened the curd will keep for 2–3 weeks: once opened, use within a week.

Cook smart
- Make lime curd by using 2 juicy limes instead of the lemon.

Mango and Apricot Chutney

There's nothing to beat home-made chutney, but not everyone appreciates the eye-smarting, vinegary fumes when it is cooked conventionally on the hob. This fruity chutney uses dried fruit to soak up the excess liquid.

Cooking time: 4 hours

Makes one 300 g/11 oz jar

- 2 firm ripe mangoes
- 75 ml/3 fl oz/5 tbsp white wine vinegar
- 150 g/5 oz/²⁄₃ cup soft light brown sugar
- 2 cm/³⁄₄ in piece of fresh root ginger, peeled and grated

- 50 g/2 oz/¹⁄₃ cup no-need-to-soak dried apricots, chopped
- a pinch of salt

1 Peel the mangoes and remove the stones (pits). Cut the flesh into small dice. Put in the ceramic cooking pot with the vinegar, then switch on the slow cooker to High. Cover with the lid and cook for 2 hours, stirring half-way through cooking.

2 Add the sugar, ginger, apricots and salt. Stir until the sugar has dissolved, then re-cover and cook for a further 2 hours or until the chutney is thick and pulpy. Stir once or twice towards the end of the cooking time to ensure the chutney does not stick.

3 Turn off the slow cooker and leave to cool for a few minutes. Spoon the chutney into hot sterilised jars and seal.

4 Store in a cool, dry place for up to 3 months. Once opened, keep in the fridge and use within 3 weeks.

Whisky Marmalade

It isn't possible to make marmalade entirely in the slow cooker as it needs to boil fiercely to reach setting point. However, the slow and constant temperature is ideal for the initial softening of the citrus peel and ensures it is beautifully tender.

🕐 **Cooking time: 2¼ hours**   👥 **Makes about 700 g/1½ lb**

- 1 small lemon, halved
- 2 oranges, preferably Seville, halved
- 300 ml/½ pt/1¼ cups water

- 450 g/1 lb/2 cups granulated sugar
- 30 ml/2 tbsp whisky

1 Squeeze the juice from the lemon and oranges and place in the ceramic cooking pot, reserving the pips, pith and peel.

2 Shred the peel finely into strips about 1 cm x 3 mm/½ x ⅛ in (if the pith is very thick, trim some off to leave a 5 mm/¼ in layer on the peel). Add the peel to the cooking pot with the water. Tie the pips and pith in a piece of muslin (cheesecloth) and add as well.

3 Turn on the slow cooker to High. Cover with a lid and cook for 2 hours or until the peel is really soft.

4 Tip the mixture into a heavy-based saucepan, add the sugar and heat gently, stirring, until dissolved. Bring to the boil and boil rapidly for 15 minutes or until setting point is reached (see below).

5 Take off the heat, remove the muslin bag and leave to stand for 15 minutes. Add the whisky and stir to mix in and to distribute the peel evenly.

6 Spoon into hot sterilised jars and seal. Store in a cool, dry place for up to 6 months. Once opened, keep in the fridge and use within 3 weeks.

Cook smart

● Choose firm, ripe unwaxed citrus fruit for this recipe. You need a total weight of about 225 g/8 oz.

● To test for a set, either use a sugar thermometer – the preserve is ready when the temperature registers 105°C/220°F – or spoon a little of the marmalade on to a chilled saucer. Push a finger across; if the surface of the marmalade wrinkles, it has reached setting point.

Index

Recipes followed by (V) are vegetarian.
Page numbers in *italics* are cooking tips